Access 97

fast & easy™

How to Order:

For information on quantity discounts contact the publisher: Prima Publishing, P.O. Box 1260BK, Rocklin, CA 95677-1260; (916) 632-4400. On your letterhead include information concerning the intended use of the books and the number of books you wish to purchase. For individual orders, turn to the back of this book for more information.

Access 97

fast & easy™

Patrice-Anne Rutledge

PRIMA PUBLISHING

Prima Publishing and colophon are registered trademarks of Prima Communications, Inc. Visual Learning Guides and Fast & Easy are trademarks of Prima Publishing, a division of Prima Communications, Inc., Rocklin, California 95677.

Publisher: Matthew H. Carleson

Managing Editor: Dan J. Foster

Acquisitions Editor: Deborah F. Abshier

Development Editor: Kelli R. Crump

Project Editor: Kevin W. Ferns

Copy Editor: Judy A. Ohm

Technical Reviewer: Ray Link

Interior Design and Layout: Marian Hartsough

Cover Design: Prima Design Team

Indexer: Katherine Stimson

ISBN: 0-7615-1363-9

Library of Congress Catalog Card Number: 97-75515

Printed in the United States of America

99 HH 10 9 8 7 6 5 4 3 2

To the memory of my grandparents, Violet and August Sylvia.

Thanks for all your love, support, and encouragement.

Acknowledgments

I'd like to thank all the people at Prima Publishing who contributed to the creation of *Access 97 Fast & Easy*: Debbie Abshier, for suggesting that I write this book; Kevin Ferns and Kelli Crump, for their many organizational and editorial contributions; and Judy Ohm and Ray Link, for their attention to detail.

And special thanks to my Mom, Phyllis Rutledge, for both her editorial expertise and her encouragement throughout this project.

About the Author

Patrice-Anne Rutledge is a computer consultant and author based near San Francisco. She has written on a variety of topics, including technology, business, and travel, and has authored or co-authored twelve computer books on topics such as Microsoft Office and Microsoft Publisher. Most recently, she co-authored *The Essential Publisher 97 Book*, also published by Prima. As both an independent consultant and a member of the IS team for various international technology firms, Patrice has been involved in many aspects of computing, including software development, systems analysis, and technical communications. Patrice initially discovered computers while pursuing a career as a technical translator, and was quickly hooked. She holds a degree in French Linguistics from the University of California, and has been working with Access for more than five years.

Contents
at a Glance

PART V
CREATING AND USING FORMS 125

PART VI
QUERYING FOR INFORMATION 207

PART VII
WORKING WITH REPORTS 249

PART VIII
WORKING WITH THE WEB 295

PART IX
APPENDIXES 327

Contents

PART VII
WORKING WITH REPORTS 249

PART IX
APPENDIXES 327

Introduction

Access 97 is one of the world's most popular relational database systems, and is part of the Microsoft Office 97 professional edition. Using Access, you can create sophisticated and powerful databases to store and analyze information on a number of topics. For many beginning computer users, however, database programs seem complicated and intimidating. But they needn't be.

Access 97 Fast & Easy isn't designed to provide comprehensive coverage on every aspect of Access. Instead, it focuses on the best way to do essential tasks and then provides step-by-step visual instructions on how to do those tasks. Using this approach, creating a database is fast and easy.

WHO SHOULD READ THIS BOOK?

Access 97 Fast & Easy is a visual learning guide created for people who learn best by seeing a visual representation of what they're doing. This book is directed at beginning to intermediate computer users, particularly those new to Access 97. More experienced users who prefer a visual, hands-on approach may also benefit from this book. If you want to "look and learn" without having to wade through a lot of text and technical detail, this book is for you.

ADDED ADVICE TO MAKE YOU A PRO

Access 97 Fast & Easy provides a step-by-step, sequential approach to learning. Starting at the very beginning, the book guides you through the creation of an entire relational database system. Along the way, you'll discover several elements that will help increase your knowledge and proficiency:

✦ **Tips** provide hints on ways to make common tasks even easier, or suggest shortcuts for these tasks.

✦ **Notes** offer useful background information, advice, or suggestions that will help you learn more about the applications.

✦ **Cautions** keep you on your toes by notifying you of potential pitfalls and hazards that might hinder your progress.

Finally, the appendixes will help you expand on what you learn. In Appendix A, you'll discover how to create and print mailing labels; in Appendix B, you'll learn how to import data from Excel, another popular Office 97 program.

I hope you enjoy reading and using *Access 97 Fast & Easy*!

Patrice-Anne Rutledge

P A R T I
Getting Started

roduc

duct

roduct ID

duct Name

Supplier

Category

uantity Per Unit

Unit Price

Units In Stock

Units On Order

1 Welcome to Access 97

Access 97 is one of the most popular and powerful database applications available. Using Access, you can easily create a relational database that includes data entry forms, reports, and queries. In this chapter, you'll learn how to:

✦ Start Access

✦ Exit Access

STARTING ACCESS

Depending on the options you choose when you install Access 97, the menu path you use to start Access may differ slightly.

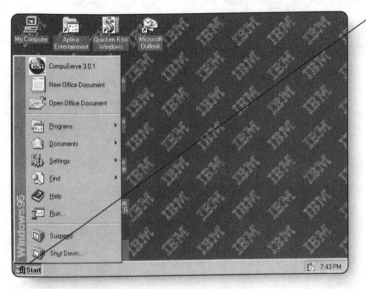

1. **Click** on the **Start button**, located in the lower-left corner of the screen. The Start menu will appear.

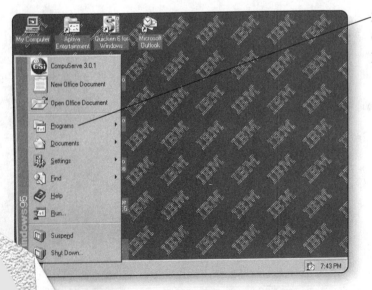

2. **Click** on **Programs**. A cascading menu of available programs will appear.

3. Click on **Microsoft Access**.

The Microsoft Access window will open.

EXITING ACCESS

When you finish working in Access, you need to exit the program properly to avoid damaging your database.

1. Click on **File**. The File menu will appear.

2a. Click on **Exit**. Access 97 will close and you will return to the Windows 95 desktop.

OR

2b. Click on the **Close button** as an alternate way to exit Access 97 in only one step.

NOTE

If you haven't saved everything in your database, Access will prompt you to do this by displaying a dialog box that asks whether you want to save your changes. Click on Yes to save the changes; click on No to discard the changes.

2 Working with Access 97

Before you create your first Access database, you need to know how to use toolbars, menus, dialog boxes, and get help when you need it. Fortunately, all of this will be familiar if you already use other Windows 95 programs, particularly other Office 97 applications. In this chapter, you'll learn how to:

✦ Use menus

✦ Use toolbars

✦ Work with dialog boxes

✦ Get help using Access

USING MENUS

You need to issue commands in order to use Access 97. The *menu bar*, directly below the Access *title bar*, includes several menu names that open groups of *menu commands*. Depending on where you are in Access and what you're doing, the menu structure will change, providing appropriate menu options.

Opening a Menu

1. **Click** on the **menu name** you want to open. A cascading menu of available commands will appear.

2. **Click** on the **menu command** you want to perform.

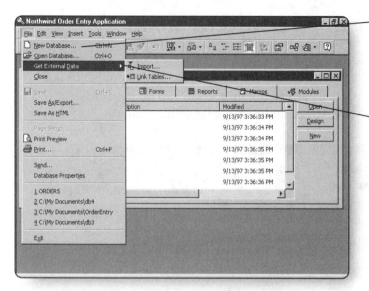

When you click on a menu command that is followed by an ellipsis (. . .), a dialog box will open.

When you click on a menu command that is followed by a right arrow, another menu will appear. Then, click on a command in that menu to perform it.

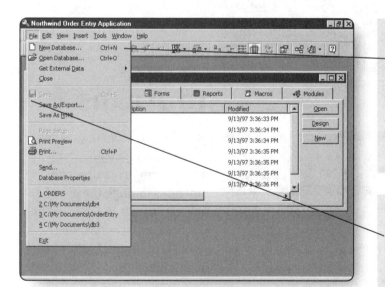

TIP

Many Access menu commands have *shortcut keys*. A shortcut key lets you bypass the menu by pressing a keyboard command such as Ctrl+N.

NOTE

Sometimes menu commands appear dimmed. This means they aren't available to use at this time. For example, the Save command on the File menu will appear dimmed if you haven't created new data.

Using a Shortcut Menu

Access offers a special kind of menu called a *shortcut menu*. A shortcut menu displays the specific menu commands that apply to a particular item you select. This item can be text, a graphic object, a row, or a column, for example.

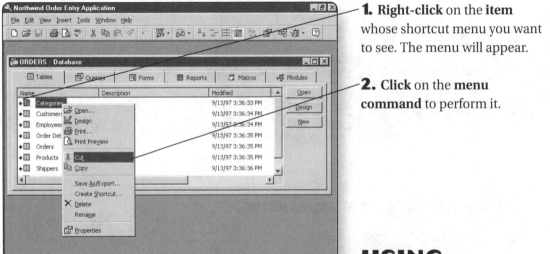

1. **Right-click** on the **item** whose shortcut menu you want to see. The menu will appear.

2. **Click** on the **menu command** to perform it.

USING TOOLBARS

In Access 97, *toolbars* give you easy access to the program's most common features and functions through the use of *toolbar buttons.* If you use other Office 97 applications, such as Word 97 or Excel 97, some of these toolbars and buttons may look familiar; there are many similarities among the Office 97 product suites. When you click on a toolbar button, you either perform a command or open a dialog box.

When Access 97 displays a database window, you see the Database toolbar. As you open individual tables, queries, forms, and reports within that database, the toolbars change. For example, when you open a table, the Table Datasheet toolbar displays and the Database toolbar disappears.

Finding Out What a Toolbar Button Does

You can use the Access Screen-Tips feature to find out what a particular toolbar button does.

Hover the mouse over the button without clicking on it. A ScreenTip will appear describing what the button does.

TIP

If a toolbar button is dimmed, it isn't available for use. For example, you must select something before the Cut and Copy buttons are available.

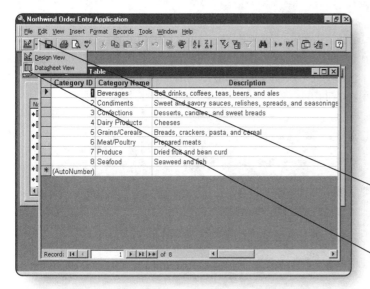

Using Toolbar Buttons That Display Menus

Some toolbar buttons, such as the View button, include a down arrow (▼) to the right of the button that opens a menu.

1. Click on the **down arrow (▼)** next to the toolbar button. A menu will appear.

2. Click on a **command** from this menu to perform it.

WORKING WITH DIALOG BOXES

When you click on a menu command followed by an ellipsis (. . .), a dialog box opens. The name of the dialog box appears in the title bar.

Dialog boxes can contain any of the following elements:

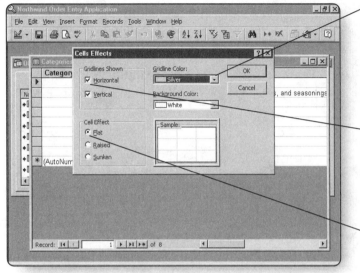

✦ **List box.** Click on the down arrow (▼) next to the list box. A list of options will appear. In a long list, you can use the up and down arrows to scroll through the list box options.

✦ **Check box.** Click to put a check mark (✔) in a check box to select that option. You can select more than one check box in a group of check boxes.

✦ **Option button.** Click on the option button to select that option. You can only select one option in a group of option buttons.

✦ **Command button.** Click on a command button to perform the command. A command button that includes an ellipsis (. . .) will open a secondary dialog box.

✦ **Scroll box.** Click on an option in the scroll box to select it.

✦ **Text box.** Enter data or information in a text box.

✦ **Preview area.** Look at the preview area to view how your choices will appear.

♦ **Help button**. Click on the Help button to activate ScreenTips help.

♦ **Close button.** Click on the Close button to close the dialog box.

♦ **Tab.** Click on a Tab to move to another sheet in the dialog box.

GETTING HELP

Access 97 provides several ways of getting help if you have a problem using the program. These help features include:

✦ Office Assistant

✦ Help Index

✦ What's This?

Using the Office Assistant

Office Assistant is an Access 97 feature that appears automatically. It provides context-sensitive help and lets you ask questions about a task you want to perform.

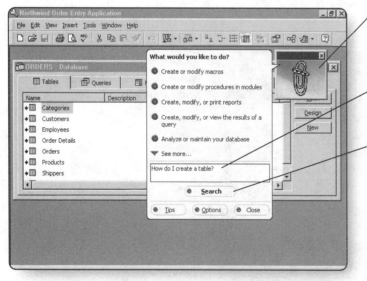

1. **Click** on the **Office Assistant**. The Office Assistant message balloon will appear.

2. **Enter** a **specific question** in the text box.

3. **Click** on **Search**. A new topic list will appear that relates to this question.

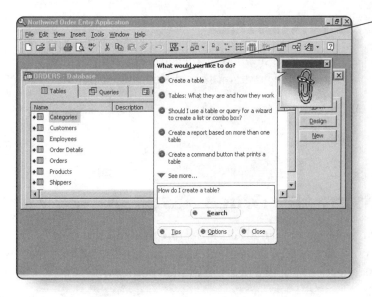

4. Click on the **topic** you want to see. Online help for this topic will appear.

5. Click on the **Close button** when you are done reading the online help.

NOTE

To turn off the Office Assistant, click on its Close button. To turn the Office Assistant back on again, click on the Office Assistant button or press F1.

Using the Help Index

You can also search the Help Index for the exact term or topic you're looking for.

1. Click on **Help**. The Help menu will appear.

2. Click on **Contents and Index**. The Help Topics: Microsoft Access 97 dialog box will open.

3. Click on the **Index tab**. A complete help index will appear.

4. Enter the **topic** you want to search for in the text box. The index will move to this entry.

5. Double-click on the index **entry** you want. The Topics Found dialog box will open.

6. Double-click on the specific **topic** you want to read.

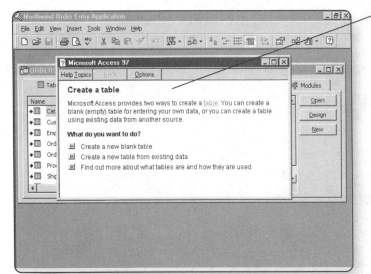

The topic will appear in the help window.

NOTE

The Help window you display using the Help Index is the same window you will find using the Office Assistant. It's just a different way to access the same information.

Using What's This? to Get Help

Access 97 includes a feature called What's This? Using this feature, you can access a ScreenTip for a menu command, toolbar button, or other item on the screen.

1. Click on **Help**. The Help menu will appear.

2. Click on **What's This?** What's This? will activate by placing a question mark next to the mouse pointer.

3. Click on the toolbar button, menu command, or part of the screen on which you want help.

A ScreenTip will appear, providing basic information.

Using What's This? in a Dialog Box

You can also access What's This? in a dialog box, but the steps are a little different.

1. **Click** on the **? button** (question mark) in the upper-right corner of the dialog box to activate What's This?

2. **Click** on the **part** of the **dialog box** on which you need help. The ScreenTip will appear.

PART I REVIEW QUESTIONS

1. How do you open Access 97? *See "Starting Access" in Chapter 1*

2. What are the two ways to exit Access? *Jump to "Exiting Access" in Chapter 1*

3. When does Access prompt you to save your database? *Flip to "Exiting Access" in Chapter 1*

4. What is the best way to navigate Access? *Accelerate to "Using Menus" in Chapter 2*

5. Which menu lets you see commands that apply only to the item you select? *Glance through "Using Shortcut Menus" in Chapter 2*

6. What's a ScreenTip? *Try "Finding Out What a Toolbar Button Does" in Chapter 2*

7. What happens when a menu command is followed by an ellipsis? *Slide to "Working with Dialog Boxes" in Chapter 2*

8. What help option lets you ask questions about the task you want to perform? *Skip back to "Using the Office Assistant" in Chapter 2*

9. How can you search for a specific topic? *Browse through "Using the Help Index" in Chapter 2*

10. What's "What's This?" *Flip to "Using What's This? to Get Help" in Chapter 2*

PART II

Creating Databases

rod

duct

roduct ID
oduct Name
Supplie
Categor
uantity Per Uni
Unit Price
Units In Stock
Units On Orde

3

Creating a Database

U sing the Access 97 Database Wizard, you can quickly create detailed databases that handle a number of business and personal functions such as order entry, contact management, or household inventory. If none of the database templates in the Database Wizard suits your needs or if you just want to create a database from scratch, you can easily do so as well. In this chapter, you'll learn how to:

✦ Start the Database Wizard

✦ Use the Database Wizard

✦ Create a Blank Database when you first start Access

✦ Create a Blank Database from within Access

STARTING THE DATABASE WIZARD WHEN YOU FIRST BEGIN ACCESS

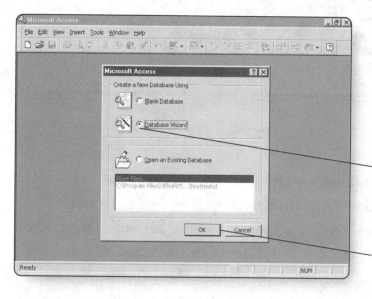

When you first start Access, you can create a database using the Database Wizard option in the Microsoft Access dialog box. This dialog box automatically appears when you start the program.

1. **Click** on the **Database Wizard option button** in the initial Microsoft Access dialog box.

2. **Click** on **OK**. The New dialog box will open.

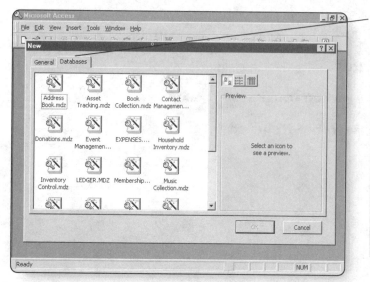

Icons for the available database templates will appear under the Databases tab.

TIP

If you can't use an Access wizard, it may not be installed. To reinstall all wizards, run Office 97 Setup again and choose the Access Wizards and Advanced Wizards options.

STARTING THE DATABASE WIZARD FROM WITHIN ACCESS

If you are already working in Access, you will follow slightly different steps to start the Database Wizard.

1. **Click** on the **New Database button**. The New dialog box will open.

2. **Click** on the **Databases tab**. Icons for the available database templates will appear.

USING THE DATABASE WIZARD

The Database Wizard guides you through the creation of a database including choosing a database template, selecting fields, making customizations, adding pictures, and finishing the database.

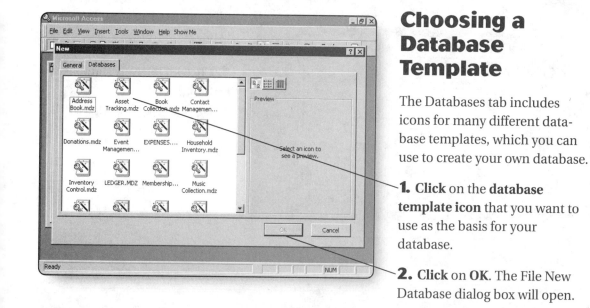

Choosing a Database Template

The Databases tab includes icons for many different database templates, which you can use to create your own database.

1. **Click** on the **database template icon** that you want to use as the basis for your database.

2. **Click** on **OK**. The File New Database dialog box will open.

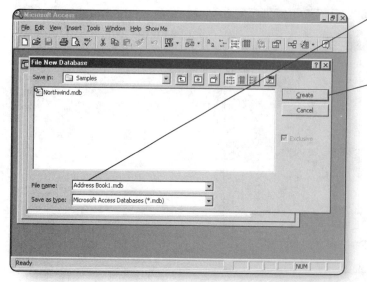

3. **Enter** a **name** for the new database in the File Name: list box.

4. **Click** on **Create**. The Database Wizard will open.

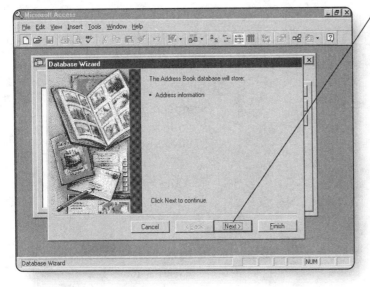

5. Click on **Next** to continue.

Selecting Database Fields

A database can contain one or more tables, each with numerous fields. The fields you'll probably want to have in your tables are already selected. Additional fields that you may want to consider aren't automatically selected and are listed in italics.

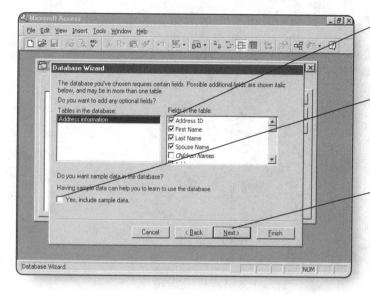

1. Click on the **check box** next to any additional field you want to include in your table.

2. Click on the **Yes, include sample data check box** to include sample data in your database.

3. Click on **Next** to continue.

> ## TIP
>
> Sample data can make it easier to learn how to use the database you've just created. Once you've viewed the database with the sample data, you can delete it and add your own.

Customizing the Database

Next, you'll customize your database by choosing styles for screens and reports. You'll also add a title.

1. Click on the **style** you want to use in database screens.

2. Click on **Next** to continue.

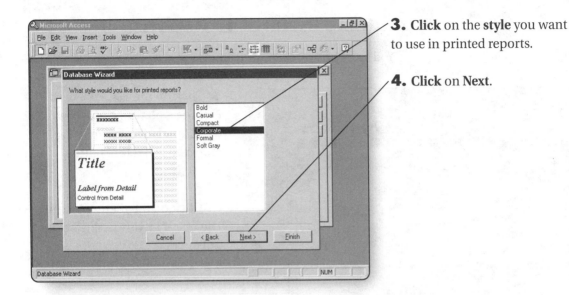

3. **Click** on the **style** you want to use in printed reports.

4. **Click** on **Next**.

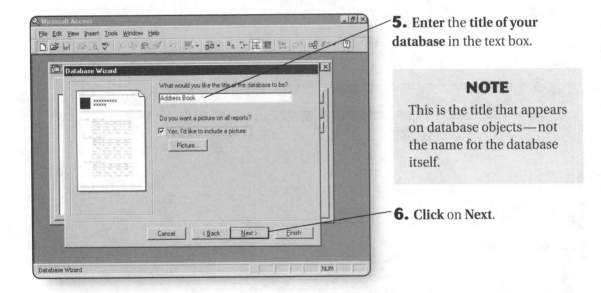

5. **Enter** the **title of your database** in the text box.

NOTE

This is the title that appears on database objects—not the name for the database itself.

6. **Click** on **Next**.

Adding Pictures to Reports

You can also add pictures to your reports.

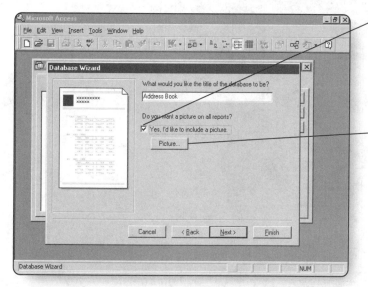

1. Click on the **Yes, I'd like to include a picture check box** to include a picture on your reports. The Picture button will activate.

2. Click on the **Picture button**. The Insert Picture dialog box will open.

3. Click on the **picture** you want to insert.

4. Click on **OK**.

5. Click on **Next** to continue.

Finishing the Database

1. Click on the **Yes, start the database check box** to start the database when you finish the Database Wizard.

2. Click on the **Display Help on using a database check box** to activate online help when you begin using the database.

3. Click on **Finish**. The Database Wizard will build the database.

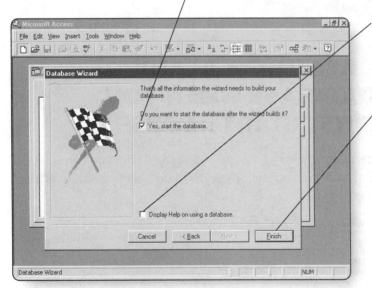

Viewing Your Database

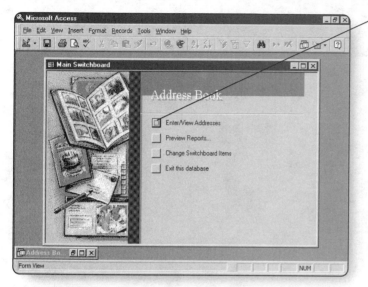

A database you build with the Database Wizard displays a form called the Main Switchboard. This form includes buttons that help you navigate around your database without having to use the main database window. Using the main switchboard, you can:

✦ Enter and view data using forms

✦ Preview reports

✦ Change switchboard items

✦ Exit the database

Although using a database with a main switchboard can be useful, especially if you're new to Access, you can also manually create a database to have complete flexibility over its design.

CREATING A BLANK DATABASE WHEN YOU FIRST START ACCESS

If you don't want to use the Database Wizard, you can create a database from scratch. You can create a blank database when you first start Access.

1. Click on the **Blank Database option button** in the initial Microsoft Access dialog box.

2. Click on **OK**. The File New Database dialog box will open.

3. Click on the **folder** in which you want to store your new database.

4. Enter an **appropriate name** for the database in the File Name: text box.

5. Click on **Create**. A blank database will appear in your Access 97 window.

CREATING A BLANK DATABASE FROM WITHIN ACCESS

If you are already working in Access, you will follow slightly different steps to create a blank database.

1. Click on the **New button**. The New dialog box will open.

2. Double-click on the **Blank Database icon** on the General tab. The File New Database dialog box will open.

3. Continue with **steps 3** through **5** in the previous listing.

Once you create a blank database, you can then create tables for it and later forms, queries, and reports.

4 Opening and Using Databases

Once you create a database in Access 97, you'll want to open it again and again. You'll also need to familarize yourself with the database window before you start working with tables, reports, queries, and forms within the database. In this chapter, you'll learn how to:

✦ Open an Existing Database

✦ Understand the Database Window

✦ Use the Database Window

OPENING AN EXISTING DATABASE

From the initial Microsoft Access dialog box that appears, you can open an existing Access database.

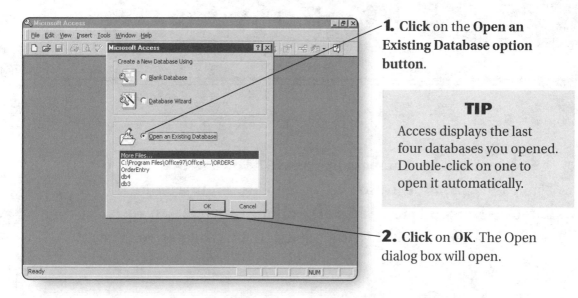

1. Click on the **Open an Existing Database option button**.

TIP

Access displays the last four databases you opened. Double-click on one to open it automatically.

2. Click on **OK**. The Open dialog box will open.

3. Click on the **folder** that contains the database you want to open.

4. Double-click on the **database filename** you want to open. The database will appear in the Access 97 window.

> **NOTE**
>
> You can open several existing sample databases included with Access 97 to get ideas on how to create your own. You will find these sample databases in the C:\Program Files \Microsoft Office\Office \Samples folder if you followed the standard setup.

UNDERSTANDING THE DATABASE WINDOW

The Access database window includes six tabs, each corresponding to one of the six *objects* that make up an Access *database*. A *database* is essentially a collection of information. In an Access database, you collect information in tables, enter information into these tables by using forms, query tables to analyze their content, and then create reports based on the tables and queries.

USING THE DATABASE WINDOW

After you open a database, you can open or create tables, reports, queries, and forms.

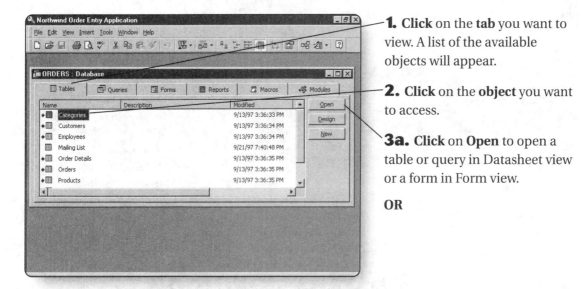

1. Click on the **tab** you want to view. A list of the available objects will appear.

2. Click on the **object** you want to access.

3a. Click on **Open** to open a table or query in Datasheet view or a form in Form view.

OR

3b. Click on **Preview** to preview a report.

OR

3c. Click on **Design** to display the object in Design view.

OR

3d. Click on **New** to create a new database object. The New dialog box will open.

PART II REVIEW QUESTIONS

1. Which wizard helps you to automatically create a database? *Cast your eyes on "Starting the Database Wizard When You First Begin Access" in Chapter 3*

2. What is an alternative way to start the Database Wizard? *Pay attention to "Starting the Database Wizard from Within Access" in Chapter 3*

3. How do you use database templates? *Look over "Choosing a Database Template" in Chapter 3*

4. Where can you choose styles for screens and reports? *Consider "Customizing the Database" in Chapter 3*

5. What is a main switchboard? *See "Viewing Your Database" in Chapter 3*

6. If you're already working in Access, how do you create a database from scratch? *Scratch the surface in "Creating a Blank Database from Within Access" in Chapter 3*

7. After you've saved a database, how do you open it again? *Remember in "Opening an Existing Database" in Chapter 4*

8. What is a database? *Find out in "Understanding the Database Window" in Chapter 4*

9. What are the six tabs in the database window? *Jump to "Understanding the Database Window" in Chapter 4*

10. What are three things you can do in the database window? *Look through "Using the Database Window" in Chapter 4*

PART III

Working with Tables

rodu

ducts

roduct ID:

duct Name:

Supplier:

Category:

uantity Per Unit:

Unit Price:

Units In Stock:

Units On Order:

5 Creating a Table with the Table Wizard

The Access 97 Table Wizard offers a fast and easy way to create your own tables. Access includes numerous table templates that you can use to create both business and personal database tables and provides step-by-step guidance as you do so. In this chapter, you will learn how to:

✦ Start the Table Wizard

✦ Choose table fields

✦ Name the table and set a key

✦ Set table relationships

✦ Finish the table

STARTING THE TABLE WIZARD

The Table Wizard can help you create common types of tables, including those that store mailing lists, recipes, investments, video collections, invoices, or exercise logs.

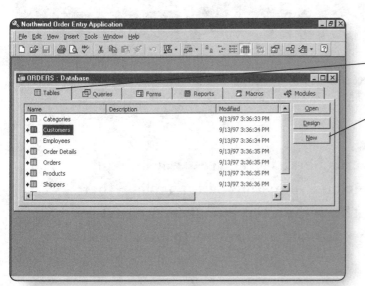

1. **Click** on the **Tables tab** in the main database window.

2. **Click** on **New**. The New Table dialog box will open.

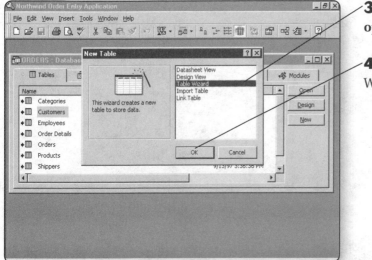

3. **Click** on the **Table Wizard option**.

4. **Click** on **OK**. The Table Wizard will appear.

CHOOSING TABLE FIELDS

Next, you choose the specific fields for your table. You can easily modify the sample tables by selecting only certain fields or by renaming the fields to something that's more appropriate for your needs.

1a. **Click** on the **Business option button**. Sample business tables will appear in the Sample Tables: scroll box.

OR

1b. **Click** on the **Personal option button**. Sample personal tables will appear in the Sample Tables: scroll box.

2. **Scroll down** the Sample Tables: scroll box until you see the sample table you want to use.

3. **Click** on this **sample table**. Sample fields, based on the table you choose, will appear in the Sample Fields: scroll box.

4. Click on the **sample field** from the Sample Fields: scroll box that you want to include in your table. The field will be selected.

5. Click on the **right arrow button**. The sample field will move to the Fields in My New Table: scroll box.

6. Repeat steps 3, 4, and 5 until you've selected all the sample fields you want to include in your table.

7. Click on Next. The Table Wizard will continue to the next step.

TIP

Click on the double right arrow to include all sample fields in your table.

Removing Fields

You can easily remove fields you selected to include in your new table.

1. Scroll down the Fields in My New Table: scroll box until you see the field you want to remove.

2. Click on this **field.** The field will be selected.

3. Click on the **left arrow button**. The field will be removed from the Fields in My New Table: scroll box.

TIP

Click on the double left arrow to remove all the fields in the Fields in My New Table: scroll box.

Renaming Fields

You can rename a field after you move it to the Fields in My New Table: scroll box.

1. Click on the **field** you want to rename in the Fields in My New Table: scroll box.

2. Click on **Rename Field**. The Rename Field dialog box will open.

3. Enter the **new name** for the field in the Rename Field: text box.

4. Click on **OK**. You will return to the Table Wizard.

NAMING THE TABLE AND SETTING A KEY

In this step of the Table Wizard, you name your table and determine how to set a primary key. A *primary key* is an important concept in relational database design. This key provides a unique tag for each row in your table, called a *record*. Access uses this primary key to relate the records in this table to another table in your database.

1. Enter a **name** for your table in the text box.

2. Click on the **Yes, set a primary key for me option button**. A primary key will automatically be set.

NOTE
The easiest way to set a primary key is to let Access set it for you. If you want to set your own key, click on the No, I'll set the primary key option button. The Table Wizard opens a new dialog box in which you can choose how to set the primary key yourself.

3. Click on **Next** to continue to the next step.

TIP
A table name can have up to 64 characters including letters, numbers, and spaces. Creating meaningful names for all parts of your database—tables, reports, forms, and queries—will help make it easier to use and manage.

SETTING TABLE RELATIONSHIPS

In a relational database, you will want to relate the data from one table to another. For example, you might have a master Customers table and another table for individual Orders. You'll list each customer once in the Customers table, but list the customer many times in the Orders table as he or she places multiple orders. Each of these tables will have a field to identify the customer and it is this field that relates the tables to each other.

You will see this step only if your database already contains at least one table. If this is the first table you are creating, you will skip this step.

Click on Next if your new table isn't related to any existing tables.

If you want to relate your new table to an existing one, Access can create the relationship for you.

1. **Click** on the **name of the existing table** you want to relate to your new table.

2. **Click** on **Relationships**. The Relationships dialog box will open.

3a. **Click** on the **One record in the 'Mailing List' table will match many records in the 'Customers' table option button**.

OR

3b. **Click** on the **One record 'Customers' table will match many records in the 'Mailing List' table option button**.

NOTE

The one-to-many distinction is very important in setting table relationships. Remember that the "one record" table should be the one with unique values for that field. For example, you would list each customer once in a Customers table and many times in an Orders table.

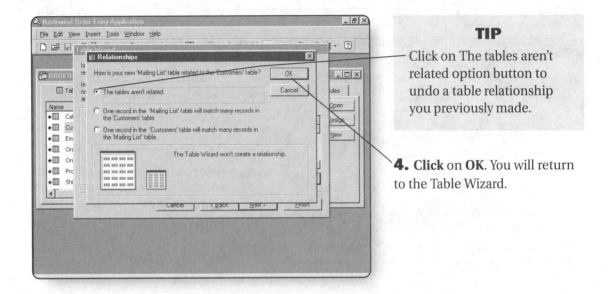

TIP

Click on The tables aren't related option button to undo a table relationship you previously made.

4. **Click** on **OK**. You will return to the Table Wizard.

5. **Click** on **Next**. You will continue to the next step.

FINISHING THE TABLE

In the last step of the Table Wizard, you determine how you want to view your completed table.

1a. **Click** on the **Modify the table design option button**. The table will open in Design view.

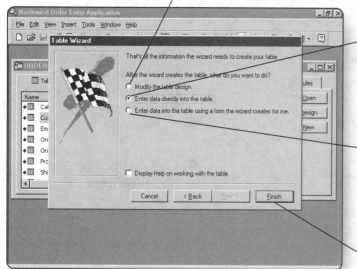

OR

1b. **Click** on the **Enter data directly into the table option button**. The table will open in Datasheet view.

OR

1c. **Click** on the **Enter data into the table using a form the wizard creates for me option button**. A form for entering data into your table will open.

2. **Click** on **Finish**.

The table will open based on your instructions in step 1.

6

Creating a Table from Scratch

If you want more control over table creation than the Table Wizard provides, or you just want to try creating a table from scratch, Access offers two different methods. In this chapter, you'll learn how to:

✦ Create a table in Datasheet View

✦ Create a table in Design View

CREATING A TABLE IN DATASHEET VIEW

If you want to create your own table without using the Table Wizard, you can create one in Datasheet View and then let Access analyze it and automatically set data types and a primary key.

When you save a table that you create in Datasheet View, Access automatically inserts an ID AutoNumber field and sets it as the primary key. Data types are set based on the types of entries you make in each column. For example, a column with currency entries will have a Currency data type. A column with only numeric entries will have a Number data type. And one with only text entries, or a mixture of text and numbers, will have a Text data type.

Even though Access automatically sets data types and the primary key when you create a table in Datasheet View, you'll probably still want to modify the field names. By default, the fields are labeled Field1, Field2, and so on, which isn't very descriptive or useful.

When choosing field names for your table, keep in mind that Access field names can only have up to 64 characters. You can include:

✦ Letters of the alphabet

✦ Numbers

✦ Special characters, except for a period, an exclamation, a grave accent, or brackets

✦ Spaces, but only if you're not planning to use the field name in an expression or Visual Basic, both advanced features of Access

1. Click on the **Tables tab** in the main database window.

2. Click on **New**. The New Table dialog box will open.

3. Click on the **Datasheet View option**.

4. Click on **OK**. A blank table will open in Datasheet View.

5. Enter the **desired data** into your table.

6. Click on the **column header** of the first column you want to rename.

7. Click on **Format**. The Format menu will appear.

8. Click on **Rename Column**. The column header name will be selected.

9. Type in a **new column name**.

10. Repeat steps 6 through **9** until you rename all necessary columns.

11. Click on the **Close button**. A dialog box will open, asking if you want to save your new table.

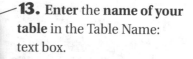

12. **Click** on **Yes**. The Save As dialog box will open.

13. **Enter** the **name of your table** in the Table Name: text box.

14. **Click** on **OK**. A dialog box will open, asking if you want to set a primary key.

15. **Click** on **Yes**. The main database window will display.

You can now open your new table in Design View to look at the automatic defaults as well as make any additional modifications.

> **TIP**
>
> By default, a table you create in Datasheet View includes 20 fields. If you don't need all these fields, you can delete unnecessary fields by selecting them and choosing the Edit, Delete Column.

CREATING A TABLE IN DESIGN VIEW

To gain even more control over how you create your table, you can create it in Design View. In Design View, you enter your own field names and descriptions and choose your own data type to associate with each field. You also set your own primary key.

Before creating a table entirely from scratch, you should write down your basic table structure on paper, focusing particularly on field names and data types. Access fields can have one of the following data types:

✦ **Text**. Stores text or combinations of text and numbers—such as addresses—up to 255 characters.

✦ **Memo**. Stores text and numbers with up to 64,000 characters; used for detailed, descriptive fields.

+ **Number**. Stores numeric data that you can use in calculations.

+ **Date/Time**. Stores a field in date or time format.

+ **Currency**. Stores currency data that you can use in calculations.

+ **AutoNumber**. Stores a sequential number for each record.

+ **Yes/No**. Stores only one of two values such as Yes/No, True/False, or On/Off.

+ **OLE Object**. Stores objects created in another application—such Word 97 or Excel 97—that you can link to or embed in an Access table.

+ **Hyperlink**. Stores a link to a UNC or URL, such as a page on the World Wide Web.

+ **Lookup Wizard**. Stores a lookup column that you can use as a lookup in another table.

1. **Click** on the **Tables tab** in the main database window.

2. **Click** on **New**. The New Table dialog box will open.

3. **Click** on the **Design View option**.

4. **Click** on **OK**. A blank table will open in Design View.

5. **Enter** the **first field name** in the Field Name column.

6. **Tab** to the **Data Type column**.

7. **Click** on the **down arrow (▼)** to the right of the field. A list of available data types will appear.

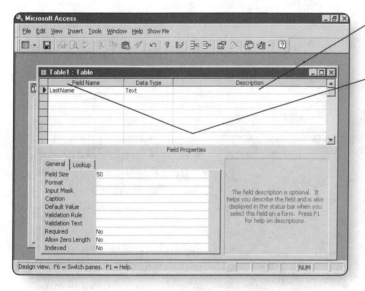

8. **Click** on the **desired data type**.

9. **Tab** to the **Description column**.

10. **Enter** a **description of this field**.

11. **Tab** back to the **Field Name column**.

12. **Repeat steps 5** through **11** until you finish entering fields.

Setting a Primary Key

In each new table that you create, you'll want to set one field as the *primary key*. A primary key is a field that is unique in each record of your table. Access uses this key to relate this table's records to those in another table.

1. Click on the **field** that you want to set as the primary key. An arrow will appear in the field selector column.

2. Click on the **Primary Key button**.

The field will be set as the primary key, with a small key in the field selector column.

The primary key is a toggle. To remove it, select the primary key field and click on the Primary Key button again.

Setting Format Properties

Access always sets each field with the default format for its data type. This format defines how the field displays in tables, forms, and reports. You may want to change this format to one of the other options. For example, a field with a Currency data type has a format of Currency by default. By changing the format, however, you can display this field in other ways, such as a percentage.

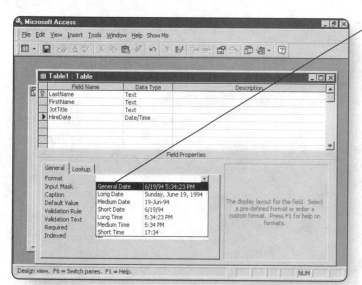

1. **Click** on the **field** whose format properties you want to set.

2. **Click** on the **General tab** in the Field Properties area.

3. **Click** on the **Format text box**. A down arrow (▼) will appear.

4. **Click** on the **down arrow** (▼) to display a list of possible formats.

5. **Click** on the **format** you want to apply.

Setting Field Size Properties for Text Fields

The default field size for a field with a data type of Text is 50 characters. You can change this size to any amount from 0 to 255 characters.

1. Click on the **field** whose field size you want to change.

2. Click on the **General tab** in the Field Properties area.

3. Enter the **new field size** in the Field Size text box.

Saving the Table

Once you finish creating your table, you'll want to save it.

1. Click on the **Close button**. A dialog box will open, asking if you want to save the table.

2. Click on **Yes**. The Save As dialog box will open.

3. Enter a **name for your table** in the Table Name: text box.

4. Click on **OK**.

The main database window will appear again.

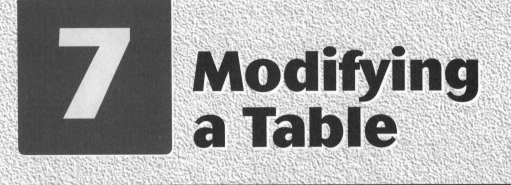

7 Modifying a Table

Once you create an Access table, you can easily modify it by adding, deleting, moving, or renaming table fields. In this chapter, you'll learn how to:

✦ Open a table in Design View

✦ Insert, delete, rename, and move fields

✦ Change the data type

OPENING A TABLE IN DESIGN VIEW

To modify a table's design, you must open it in Design View.

1. **Click** on the **Tables tab** in the main database window.

2. **Click** on the **table** that you want to open. It will then be selected.

3. **Click** on the **Design button**. The table will open in Design View.

NOTE

You can also open a table in Design View directly from the Table Wizard by choosing the Modify the Table Design option button on the final wizard step.

In Design View, you see each field's underlying structure—its name, data type, description, and properties.

INSERTING A FIELD

You can insert a field in an existing table.

1. Click on the **row** beneath where you want to add a field. An arrow will appear in the field selector column.

2. Click on the **Insert Rows button**.

A blank row will be added.

DELETING A FIELD

You can easily delete a field from a table.

1. **Click** on the **field row** that you want to delete. An arrow will appear in the field selector column.

2. **Click** on the **Delete Rows button**. A warning dialog box will appear.

3. **Click** on **Yes**.

The field will be permanently deleted.

TIP

To delete more than one field at a time, select the first field and, holding down the Ctrl key, continue selecting the remaining fields you want to delete.

CAUTION

Before you delete a field, be sure to check if you've used the field in a report, form, or query somewhere else in the database.

RENAMING A FIELD

You can easily rename a field in an Access table; however, remember that renaming a field can also affect reports, forms, and queries that contain this field. If you want to rename the field in the table, you must rename it in all other objects that contain it.

1. Select the **Field Name** that you want to rename.

2. Enter the **new name**.

MOVING A FIELD

If you want to change the order of the fields in your table, you can do so.

1. **Click** on the **field row** that you want to move. An arrow will appear in the field selector column.

2. **Drag** the **field** to its new location.

The field is now positioned in this new location.

CAUTION

Remember that changing the data type of a field may restrict the types of entries you can make or may truncate existing entries.

CHANGING THE DATA TYPE

You can change the data type of existing table fields. For example, you might want to change a number field to a currency field.

1. Click on the **field** whose data type you want to change in the Data Type column.

2. Click on the **down arrow (▼)** to the right of the Data Type column in the field row whose data type you want to change. A drop-down list will appear.

3. Click on the **new data type**.

The new data type will become permanent when you save the table.

PART III REVIEW QUESTIONS

1. Which wizard automatically creates a new table? *Learn in "Starting the Table Wizard" in Chapter 5*

2. How do you change the name of a field? *See "Renaming Fields" in Chapter 5*

3. Where does Access automatically set a primary key? *Flip to "Naming the Table and Setting a Key" in Chapter 5*

4. How do you relate data from one table to another? *Make the connection in "Setting Table Relationships" in Chapter 5*

5. How do you create your own table, yet still let Access automate certain tasks for you? *Find out in "Creating a Table in Datasheet View" in Chapter 6*

6. In which view can you create a table entirely from scratch? *Pass over to "Creating a Table in Design View" in Chapter 6*

7. How do you set a unique key for each record in your table? *Unlock the secret in "Setting a Primary Key" in Chapter 6*

8. In which view can you open a table to modify it? *Discover in "Opening a Table in Design View" in Chapter 7*

9. How do you add a new field to an existing table? *Pick through "Inserting a Field" in Chapter 7*

10. Where do you change the data type of an existing table field? *File through "Changing the Data Type" in Chapter 7*

PART IV

Entering, Editing, and Viewing Data

rodu

ducts

roduct ID:

duct Name:

Supplier:

Category

uantity Per Unit:

Unit Price

Units In Stock

Units On Order

8 Entering Data

Access 97 offers two ways to enter data into tables. You can enter new data while existing data is in view, or hide the existing information while you enter data. In this chapter, you'll learn how to:

✦ Open a table in Datasheet View

✦ Use Edit mode to enter data

✦ Use Data Entry mode to enter data

OPENING A TABLE IN DATASHEET VIEW

To enter data in a table, you need to open it in Datasheet View.

1. **Click** on the **Tables tab** in the main database window.

2. **Click** on the **table** that you want to open. It will then be selected.

3. **Click** on the **Open button**. The table will open in Datasheet View.

NOTE

You can also open a table in Datasheet View directly from the Table Wizard by choosing the Enter Data Directly Into the Table option button on the final wizard step.

Datasheet View looks similar to a spreadsheet, such as Excel 97. It uses a row and column format to display table data in a series of fields. Each row is referred to as a *record*.

NAVIGATING IN DATASHEET VIEW

Access 97 identifies the current record with an arrow in the *record selector column* for that record.

The record number box at the bottom of the screen also displays the current record number. This box is surrounded by several navigation buttons that help you navigate the table. Using these buttons, you can move to the first, preceding, next, or last record.

You can also use the mouse to navigate the datasheet or select the field you want. In addition, Access also provides several other navigation commands.

Enter or Tab	Navigates to the next field.
Shift+Tab	Navigates to the preceding field.
Page Up	Navigates up one screen.
Page Down	Navigates down one screen.

USING EDIT MODE TO ENTER DATA

You can use *Edit mode* to enter data into your table. Using Edit mode, you can add records at the end of an existing table.

1. Click on the **New Record button**. A blank record will appear at the bottom of the table.

2. Enter data in the new record.

3. Tab to the **next blank record** when you finish entering data in the first.

4. Repeat steps 2 and 3 until you finish adding data.

NOTE

Access automatically enters the next consecutive number in an AutoNumber field once you tab out of it.

USING DATA ENTRY MODE TO ENTER DATA

You can also use Data Entry mode to enter data into a datasheet. Data Entry mode displays a blank table and temporarily hides all previously entered records from view.

1. Click on **Records**. The Records menu will appear.

2. Click on **Data Entry**. Data Entry mode will be activated.

3. **Enter data** in the new record.

4. **Tab** to the **next blank record** when you finish entering data in the first.

5. **Repeat steps 3** and **4** until you finish adding data.

Exiting Data Entry Mode

When you finish entering data using Data Entry mode, you can deactivate it.

1. **Click** on **Records**. The Records menu will appear.

2. Click on **Remove Filter/Sort**.

The hidden records will appear again.

9

Editing Data

You can modify or undo your last edit in Access 97. Access also includes a powerful search and replace feature that lets you quickly update large amounts of data. In this chapter, you'll learn how to:

✦ Modify data

✦ Undo edits

✦ Replace data

✦ Delete records

MODIFYING DATA

You can modify an existing table entry in Datasheet View by replacing all or part of the data.

Modifying the Entire Field Contents

You can replace the entire contents of the selected field.

1. **Place** the **mouse pointer** on the left side of the field. A large white plus sign will appear.

2. **Click** on the **field**. The entire field will be selected.

3. **Replace** the **existing field data** with new data.

Modifying Partial Field Contents

You can replace parts of the selected field contents, such as individual words.

1. Click on the **field** whose data you want to modify. The I-beam pointer will appear.

2. Replace the **desired data** with new information.

UNDOING EDITS

If you make a mistake while editing data, Access 97's Undo feature lets you undo the last edit you make. Depending upon your last action, the label for the Undo button may display Undo Typing, Undo Current Field/Record, or Undo Saved Record. If there is nothing to undo, the button label will display Can't Undo.

To use the Undo feature, click on the Undo button on the toolbar. The last edit will be undone.

CAUTION

You can only undo the last edit you make, not previous edits.

REPLACING DATA

Using the Access 97 Replace feature, you can quickly search for and replace specific data in a table open in Datasheet View. This is particularly useful with tables that contain hundreds or even thousands of records.

1. Click on a **field** in the column in which you want to replace data.

2. Click on **Edit**. The Edit menu will appear.

3. Click on **Replace**. The Replace in Field dialog box will open.

4. Enter the **text** that you want to replace in the Find What: text box.

5. Enter the **text** that you want to use as a replacement in the Replace With: text box.

6a. Choose All from the Search: drop-down list to search the entire table for your specified criteria.

OR

6b. Choose Up from the Search: drop-down list to search only the records prior to the currently selected record.

OR

6c. Choose Down from the Search: drop-down list to search only the records after the currently selected record.

NOTE

The record in which you clicked to select the search field in step 1 is the currently selected record.

7. Click on the **Match Case check box** to locate only those entries that exactly match the case in your search criteria.

8. Click on the **Match Whole Field check box** to locate only those entries whose formatting exactly matches your search criteria.

9. Click on the **Search Only Current Field check box** to search only the field you selected in step 1.

TIP

To replace fields throughout the entire table, remove the check (✔) from the Search Only Current Field check box.

10. Click on the **Replace All button** to replace all instances of the entered text.

11. **Click** on the **Close button** to exit the Replace in Field dialog box.

DELETING RECORDS

You can entirely delete records from Access tables.

1. **Click** on the **record selector column** of the record you want to delete. An arrow will appear in the column.

2. **Click** on **Edit**. The Edit menu will appear.

3. Click on **Delete Record**. A warning box will open.

4. Click on **Yes** to permanently delete the record.

TIP

You can also delete a record by clicking on the Delete Record button in the toolbar.

NOTE

You can't undo a record deletion.

10 Sorting, Filtering, and Finding Data

Access 97 includes several features that help you locate, organize, and analyze specific information in your tables while in Datasheet View. In this chapter, you'll learn how to:

✦ Sort data

✦ Filter data

✦ Find data

SORTING DATA

With a table open in Datasheet View, you can sort data in one or more fields in either ascending or descending order.

TIP

Remember that to open a table in Datasheet View, you can double-click on the table from the Tables tab in the main database window.

1. Select the **field or fields** on which you want to sort.

TIP

To sort more than one field, select the first field and then press the Shift key as you make additional selections.

2a. Click on the **Sort Ascending button** in the toolbar.

OR

2b. Click on the **Sort Descending button**.

NOTE

If you select more than one field on which to sort, Access will sort the fields in order from left to right.

Removing a Sort

After applying a sort, you can remove it and restore the default order of the table data.

1. **Click** on **Records**. The Records menu will appear.

2. **Click** on **Remove Filter/Sort**.

FILTERING DATA

Access 97's Filter by Selection feature lets you select specific data in a table open in Datasheet View and then quickly applies a basic filter. For example, if you want only to view records for customers located in California, you could click on any field containing the word "California" and then apply Filter by Selection to view these records.

1. Click on a **field** that contains the data on which you want to filter.

2. Click on the **Filter by Selection button**.

Only the records that contain this data now display. Access hides all other records.

3. Click on the **Remove Filter button** to remove the filter. The Remove Filter button becomes the Apply Filter button. Click on it again to reapply your last filter.

Filtering by Form

The Filter by Form feature lets you filter based on more than one criterion. Using this feature, you can filter based on both AND and OR criteria. If you specify AND criteria, Access will display only those records that meet *all* the specified criteria. For example, if you filter on both Entree and Dessert, only records with both criteria will display. If you filter on Entree or Dessert, then records that meet either condition will display.

1. Click on the **Filter by Form button**. The Filter by Form window will appear with the Look For tab active.

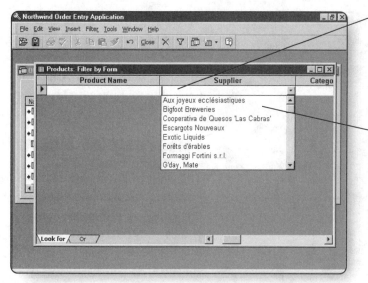

2. **Click** on the **field** on which you want to filter. A down arrow (▼) and drop-down list will appear to the right of the selected field.

3. **Choose** the **filter criterion** from the drop-down list.

4. **Repeat steps 2** and **3** until you select all desired AND criteria.

5. **Click** on the **Or tab** if you want to specify OR criteria.

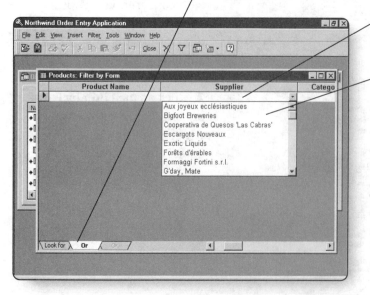

6. **Click** on the **field** on which you want to filter.

7. **Choose** the **filter criterion** from the drop-down list.

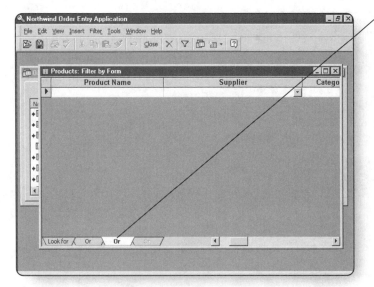

8. **Click** on the **next Or tab** if you want to specify another OR criterion.

9. **Repeat steps** **5** through **8** until you finish specifying OR criteria.

10. **Click** on the **Apply Filter button**. The filter results will appear.

11. **Click** on the **Remove Filter button** once you've viewed the filter results, which will remove the filter and restore the original data.

Saving a Filter by Form

While you are in the Filter by Form window, you can save filter by form results as a query.

1. **Click** on the **Save As Query button**. The Save As Query dialog box will open.

2. Enter a **name** in the Query Name: text box.

3. Click on **OK**.

When you want to view these filter results again, open the query from the Queries tab in the main database window.

FINDING DATA

Using the Access 97 Find feature, you can quickly search for specific data in a table open in Datasheet View. This is particularly useful with tables that contain hundreds or even thousands of records.

1. Click on the **field** in which you wish to search.

2. Click on **Edit**. The Edit menu will appear.

3. Click on **Find**. The Find in Field dialog box will open.

4. Enter the **word or words** on which you want to search in the Find What: text box.

5a. Choose All from the Search: drop-down list to search the entire table for your specified criteria.

OR

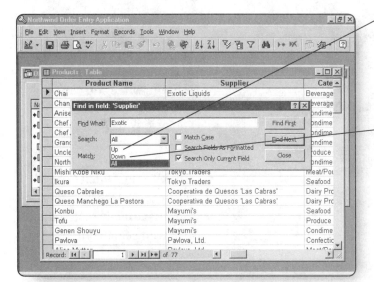

5b. Choose **Up** from the Search: drop-down list to search only the records prior to the currently selected record.

OR

5c. Choose **Down** from the Search: drop-down list to search only the records after the currently selected record.

NOTE

The currently selected record is the record in which you clicked to select the search field in step 1.

6a. Choose **Any Part of Field** from the Match: drop-down list to search for any partial match of your search criteria.

OR

6b. Choose **Whole Field** from the Match: drop-down list to search for an exact match of your search criteria.

OR

6c. Choose **Start of Field** from the Match: drop-down list to search for any entry whose initial data matches your search criteria.

TIP

Searching for only the start of the field or parts of fields is useful when you can't remember the exact entry you're looking for.

7. **Click** on the **Match Case check box** to locate only those entries that exactly match the case in your search criteria.

8. **Click** on the **Search Fields As Formatted check box** to locate only those entries whose formatting exactly matches your search criteria.

NOTE

Searching fields as formatted is useful if you want to search only for exact date formatting, for example. Entering 10/15/97 would not match with the entry October 15, 1997 if this check box is selected.

9. **Click** on the **Search Only Current Field check box** to search only the field you selected in step 1.

10. **Click** on the **Find First button** to locate the first matching entry.

11. **Click** on the **Find Next button** to display the next match.

12. **Repeat step 11** until you've viewed all desired matches.

13. **Click** on the **Close button** to exit the Find in Field dialog box.

11 Revising the Datasheet Layout

In Datasheet View, you can make many layout modifications to display the datasheet in the format that's most convenient for you. In this chapter, you'll learn how to:

✦ Resize datasheet columns and rows

✦ Freeze and unfreeze columns

✦ Hide and unhide columns

✦ Rename columns

RESIZING DATASHEET COLUMNS

In Datasheet View, you can resize the width of individual columns.

1. Click on the **column** that you want to resize. It will be selected.

2. Click on **Format**. The Format menu will appear.

3. Click on **Column Width**. The Column Width dialog box will open.

4a. **Enter** the **exact column width** in the Column Width: text box.

OR

4b. **Click** on the **Standard Width check box**. The column width will default to approximately one screen inch.

OR

4c. **Click** on the **Best Fit button**. The column width will adjust to display the headings and all field values.

5. **Click** on **OK** if the dialog box didn't automatically close by clicking on the Best Fit button.

TIP

You can also automatically set the best fit by double-clicking on the black arrow that appears when you place the mouse pointer to the right of a column header.

TIP

To manually adjust the column width, drag the black arrow to the left or right to reposition the column grid.

RESIZING DATASHEET ROWS

In Datasheet View, you can also resize row height.

1. Click on **Format**. The Format menu will appear.

2. Click on **Row Height**. The Row Height dialog box will open.

3a. **Enter** the **exact row height** in the Row Height: text box.

OR

3b. **Click** on the **Standard Height check box**. The row height will default to approximately 12.75 points.

4. **Click** on **OK**.

TIP

To manually adjust the row height, place the mouse pointer next to the record locator column and resize the row as desired.

FREEZING AND UNFREEZING COLUMNS

If you have many columns (fields) in your table, you won't be able to view the leftmost columns if you scroll to the right. If you want a column or columns to always be visible, you can freeze them. For example, in a table that contains employee information, you might always want to see employee names as you scroll across columns viewing their information.

Freezing Columns

You can freeze one or more columns.

1. **Click** on the **column header** of the first column you want to freeze.

2. **Drag** the **mouse pointer** to include other columns if you want to freeze more than one column.

3. **Click** on **Format**. The Format menu will appear.

4. **Click** on **Freeze Columns**.

A black line will appear in the grid to the right of the last frozen column.

Unfreezing Columns

If you no longer want to have the frozen columns always visible, you can unfreeze them.

1. Click on **Format**. The Format menu will appear.

2. Click on **Unfreeze All Columns**.

HIDING AND UNHIDING COLUMNS

In a large table, it can be confusing to view many extraneous fields that are important to the table structure, but convey no actual meaning. ID and AutoNumber fields are examples of this. You may also want to focus only on a few fields in your table, not all of them.

Hiding Columns

In Access 97, you can temporarily hide any columns you don't want to view.

1. Click on the **column header** of the column you want to hide.

2. Drag the **mouse pointer** to include other columns if you want to hide more than one column.

3. Click on **Format**. The Format menu will appear.

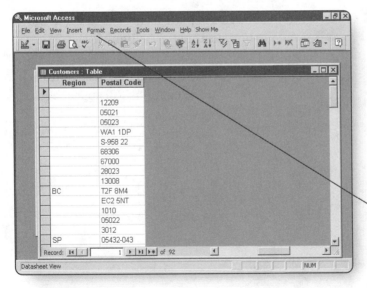

4. Click on **Hide Columns**.

The columns disappear from view, but aren't deleted.

Unhiding Columns

You'll use the Unhide Columns dialog box to select the columns you want to unhide. A check (✔) appears in the check boxes of all visible columns; hidden columns have no check.

1. Click on **Format**. The Format menu will appear.

2. Click on **Unhide Columns**. The Unhide Columns dialog box will open.

3. Click on the **check boxes** to place a check (✔) next to the columns you want to unhide from the Column: list.

4. Click on the **Close button**. The columns will appear again.

RENAMING COLUMNS

You can rename a field column directly in Datasheet View.

1. **Click** on the **column header** of the column you want to rename.

2. **Click** on **Format**. The Format menu will appear.

3. **Click** on **Rename Column**. The column header name will be selected.

4. Type in a **new column name**.

When you save the table, the new column (field) name will be permanent.

CAUTION

Before you rename a column, be sure to check if you've used the field in a report, form, or query somewhere else in the database.

NOTE

You can't rename more than one column at a time.

City	Region	Postal Code	Country	Phone	Fax
Berlin		12209	Germany	030-0074321	030-0076545
México D.F.		05021	Mexico	(5) 555-4729	(5) 555-3745
México D.F.		05023	Mexico	(5) 555-3932	
London		WA1 1DP	UK	(171) 555-7788	(171) 555-6750
Luleå		S-958 22	Sweden	0921-12 34 65	0921-12 34 67
Mannheim		68306	Germany	0621-08460	0621-08924
Strasbourg		67000	France	88.60.15.31	88.60.15.32
Madrid		28023	Spain	(91) 555 22 82	(91) 555 91 99
Marseille		13008	France	91.24.45.40	91.24.45.41
Tsawassen	BC	T2F 8M4	Canada	(604) 555-4729	(604) 555-3745
London		EC2 5NT	UK	(171) 555-1212	
Buenos Aires		1010	Argentina	(1) 135-5555	(1) 135-4892
México D.F.		05022	Mexico	(5) 555-3392	(5) 555-7293
Bern		3012	Switzerland	0452-076545	
São Paulo	SP	05432-043	Brazil	(11) 555-7647	

PART IV REVIEW QUESTIONS

1. Which view do you use to enter data in a table? *Look at "Opening a Table in Datasheet View" in Chapter 8*

2. How can you add new records to the end of a table? *Glance through "Using Edit Mode" in Chapter 8*

3. What's the best way to enter new records while temporarily hiding existing records from view? *Feast your eyes on "Using Data Entry Mode" in Chapter 8*

4. Want to correct a mistake you made while editing a table? *Go back to "Undoing Edits" in Chapter 9*

5. What feature lets you search for and replace table data? *Gather the information in "Replacing Data" in Chapter 9*

6. Where can you filter your table data based on more than one criterion? *Flow to "Filtering by Form" in Chapter 10*

7. How can you quickly find a specific word in a table that contains thousands of records? *Needle through "Finding Data" in Chapter 10*

8. What command makes a column perpetually visible as you scroll? *Warm up to "Freezing and Unfreezing Columns" in Chapter 11*

9. How can you temporarily remove certain columns from view? *Uncover "Hiding and Unhiding Columns" in Chapter 11*

10. How do you change the name of a field column in Datasheet View? *Skip to "Renaming Columns" in Chapter 10*

PART V

Creating and Using Forms

12 Creating an AutoForm

In Access 97, the simplest and easiest way to create a form is to use the AutoForm feature. Using AutoForm, you can automatically create columnar, tabular, and datasheet forms based on a table or query you select. In this chapter, you'll learn how to:

✦ Create a Columnar AutoForm

✦ Create a Tabular AutoForm

✦ Create a Datasheet AutoForm

✦ Save and close a form

CREATING A COLUMNAR AUTOFORM

Using the AutoForm feature, you can automatically create a columnar form based on a selected table or query. In a columnar form, one record at a time will appear onscreen in a vertical format.

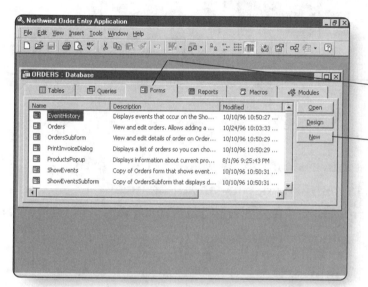

1. Click on the **Forms tab** in the main database window.

2. Click on **New**. The New Form dialog box will open.

3. Click on the **AutoForm: Columnar option**.

4. Click on the **down arrow** (▼) next to the list box. A list of choices will appear.

5. Click on the **desired table**.

6. Click on **OK**.

A columnar form based on this table will appear in Form view. You can begin entering data in the form immediately or you can modify its appearance to suit your needs.

Click on the AutoForm button on the toolbar to quickly create a columnar AutoForm based on the current open or selected table.

NOTE

An AutoForm includes all fields in the table or query on which it's based. It also defaults to the Clouds style if you select the Columnar or Tabular option. If you don't want these defaults, you can later modify the form's design or use the Form Wizard to create your form instead.

CREATING A TABULAR AUTOFORM

You can also automatically create a tabular form based on a selected table or query. The tabular format displays your table data in rows and columns.

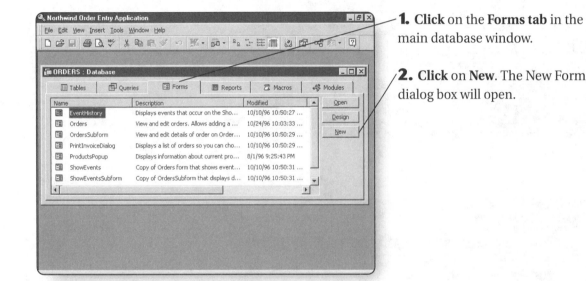

1. **Click** on the **Forms tab** in the main database window.

2. **Click** on **New**. The New Form dialog box will open.

3. **Click** on the **AutoForm: Tabular option**.

4. Click on the **down arrow (▼)** next to the list box. A list of choices will appear.

5. Click on the **desired table**.

6. Click on **OK**.

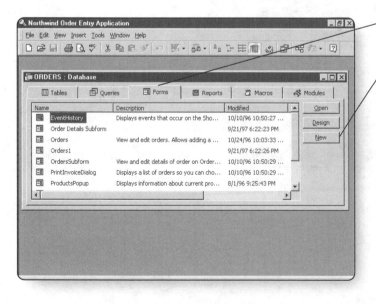

A tabular form based on this table will appear in Form view.

CREATING A DATASHEET AUTOFORM

The third AutoForm option is the Datasheet AutoForm. This type of form displays your data in the familiar Datasheet view.

1. Click on the **Forms tab** in the main database window.

2. Click on **New**. The New Form dialog box will open.

3. Click on the **AutoForm: Datasheet option**.

4. Click on the **down arrow (▼)** next to the list box. A list of choices will appear.

5. Click on the **desired table**.

6. Click on **OK**.

The form will appear in Datasheet view.

SAVING A FORM

Once you create a form, you'll want to save it.

1. Click on the **Save button**. The Save As dialog box will open.

2. Enter a **name** for your form in the Form Name: text box.

3. Click on **OK**. The form will be saved, but remain open.

Saving and Closing a Form

You can also save and close a form at the same time.

1. Click on the **Close button** on the form. A warning dialog box will open.

TIP

Click on No in the warning dialog box to close and discard the form.

2. Click on **Yes** to save the form. The Save As dialog box will open.

3. Enter a **name** for your form in the Form Name: text box.

4. Click on **OK**. The form will save and close simultaneously.

13 Creating a Form with the Form Wizard

The Access 97 Form Wizard helps you build a basic form while offering step-by-step guidance. In this chapter, you'll learn how to:

✦ Start the Form Wizard

✦ Select fields for your form

✦ Choose a form layout

✦ Choose a form style

✦ Finish the form

STARTING THE FORM WIZARD

The Form Wizard can help you select the fields, layout, and style for your form.

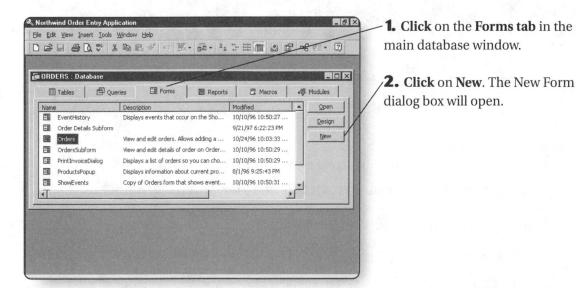

1. Click on the **Forms tab** in the main database window.

2. Click on **New**. The New Form dialog box will open.

3. Click on the **Form Wizard** option.

4. Click on **OK**. The Form Wizard will open.

SELECTING FIELDS FOR YOUR FORM

Next, you select specific fields to place in your form. Using the Form Wizard, you can select fields from more than one table or query.

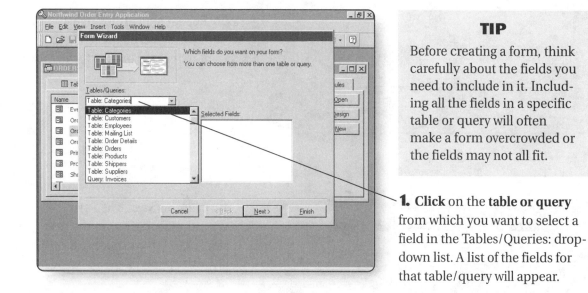

TIP

Before creating a form, think carefully about the fields you need to include in it. Including all the fields in a specific table or query will often make a form overcrowded or the fields may not all fit.

1. **Click** on the **table or query** from which you want to select a field in the Tables/Queries: drop-down list. A list of the fields for that table/query will appear.

2. **Scroll down** the **Available Fields: scroll box** until you see the first field you want to include in your form.

3. **Click** on **this field**. The field will be selected.

4. **Click** on the **right arrow button**. The field will move to the Selected Fields: list.

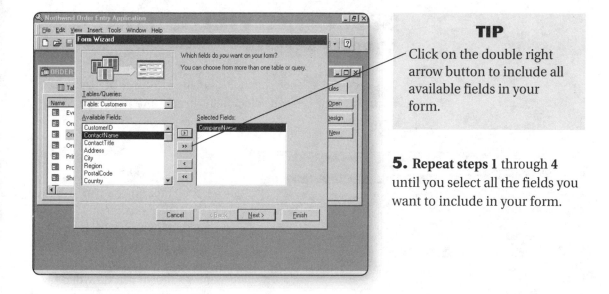

Click on the double right arrow button to include all available fields in your form.

5. Repeat steps 1 through **4** until you select all the fields you want to include in your form.

6. Click on **Next**. The Form Wizard will continue to the next step, in which you choose a layout.

CHOOSING A FORM LAYOUT

You can choose from four different form layouts in Access 97:

✦ Columnar   ✦ Tabular

✦ Datasheet   ✦ Justified

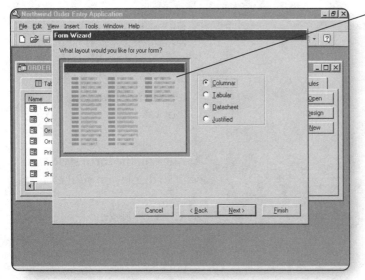

The preview box displays a sample of what the selected layout will look like.

1. **Click** on the **form layout option button** that you want to apply to your form.

2. **Click** on **Next** to continue.

CHOOSING A FORM STYLE

Access 97 includes several predefined form styles from which you can choose.

1. **Click** on the **form style** you want to display on your form.

2. **Click** on **Next**.

FINISHING THE FORM

In the final step of the Form Wizard, you enter a form title and determine how to display your finished form.

1. **Enter** the **title** you want to display on your form in the text box.

2a. **Click** on the **Open the form to view or enter information option button**. The form will open in Form View.

OR

2b. **Click** on the **Modify the form's design option button**. The form will open in Design View.

3. **Click** on the **Display Help on working with the form check box** if you want to automatically open a help window.

4. **Click** on **Finish**.

Depending on the option you selected in step 2, Access will either display the form in Form View or Design View.

— This is an example of the Form View.

Here is an example of the Design View.

14 Changing a Form's Appearance

After you create a form with the Form Wizard or AutoForm feature, you can change its default style or customize its formatting. In this chapter, you'll learn how to:

✦ Open a form in Design View

✦ Change a form's format

✦ Modify fonts

✦ Bold, italicize, and underline

✦ Set alignment

OPENING A FORM IN DESIGN VIEW

To modify the design of an existing form, open it in Design View.

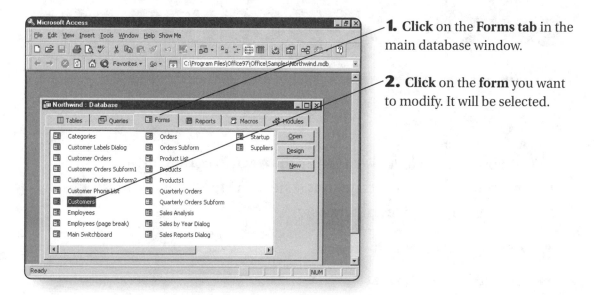

1. Click on the **Forms tab** in the main database window.

2. Click on the **form** you want to modify. It will be selected.

3. Click on the **Design button**. The form will open in Design View.

NOTE

Immediately open a form in Design View by choosing the Modify the Form's Design option button on the final Form Wizard step.

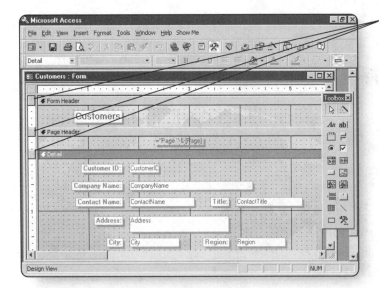

The first time you view a form in Design View, you'll notice that a form consists of *controls* placed in specific sections. Every form includes a detail section, but you can also include a form header and page header on a form.

You can also include a page footer and form footer on a form.

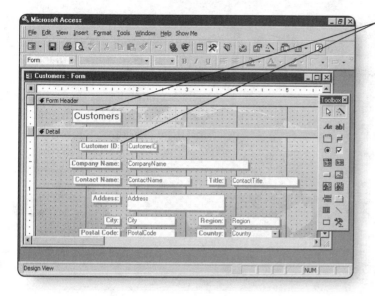

Labels and text boxes are examples of form controls. The Form Wizard and AutoForm features automatically create form sections and place controls in the appropriate location.

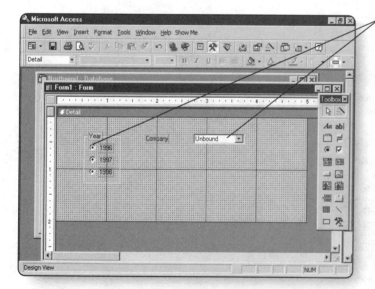

Option buttons and combo boxes are also examples of form controls. Later, you can modify form controls manually or create new ones.

TIP

If you're new to Access, it's often easier to create a new form rather than make extensive changes. Creating form controls or making major modifications to them is an advanced feature of Access.

CHANGING A FORM'S FORMAT

The Form Wizard and AutoForm features help you choose a style or AutoFormat to apply to your form. This format uses predefined colors, borders, fonts, and font sizes designed to look good together and convey a specific image. You can always change the AutoFormat if you don't like the default or the style you originally chose.

1. Click on the **AutoFormat button**. The AutoFormat dialog box will open with the current format highlighted.

2. Click on a **new form format** in the Form AutoFormats: list.

3. Click on **OK** to apply the new format.

Selecting Specific Formatting Options

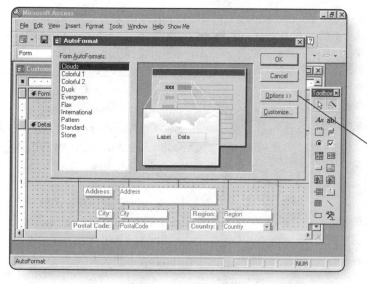

The AutoFormat default is used to apply formatting to all the fonts, colors, and borders on a form. You can also apply formatting to specific parts of the form.

1. Click on the **Options button**. The AutoFormat dialog box will extend to include the Attributes to Apply group box. By default, all attributes are selected.

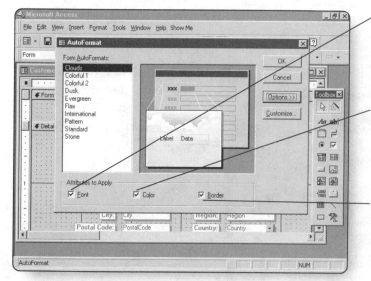

2. Click on the **Font check box** if you want to remove the ✔ and prevent formatting changes to fonts.

3. Click on the **Color check box** if you want to remove the ✔ and prevent color formatting changes.

4. Click on the **Border check box** if you want to remove the ✔ and prevent border formatting changes.

CHANGING FONTS

You can change the fonts of individual controls on a form, such as in labels or text boxes.

CAUTION

It's fun to experiment with fonts, but remember that too many different fonts on the same form can become confusing for the user.

Changing Font Style

The Font list box on the Formatting toolbar controls your form's fonts.

1. **Click** on the **control** whose font you want to change. Handles will surround this control to indicate it is selected.

NOTE

The fonts available in the Font list box can vary based on the fonts you installed in Windows 95.

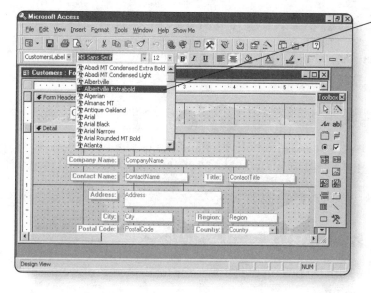

2. Choose the **new font** from the Font list box on the Formatting toolbar.

The selected control will display a new font.

Changing Font Size

The Font Size list box on the Formatting toolbar controls font size.

1. Click on the **control** whose font size you want to change. Handles will surround this control to indicate it is selected.

2. Choose the **new font size** from the Font Size list box on the Formatting toolbar.

NOTE

Font sizes range from 8 to 72 points.

The selected control will display in a new font size.

Changing Font Color

The Font/Fore Color button on the Formatting toolbar controls font color.

TIP

To apply the default color that displays on the Font/Fore Color button, click on the button.

1. Click on the **control** whose font color you want to modify. Handles will surround this control to indicate it is selected.

2. Click on the **down arrow** (▼) to the right of the Font/Fore Color button. The font color palette will open.

3. Click on the **color** you want to apply from the font color palette.

The control you selected will display a new font color.

BOLDING, ITALICIZING, AND UNDERLINING

You can also modify the appearance of a form with the bold, italics, and underline controls that contain text.

Bolding Text

The Bold button on the Formatting toolbar bolds text.

1. **Click** on the **control** that you want to bold. It will be selected.

2. **Click** on the **Bold button**.

The text will be bold.

Italicizing Text

The Italic button on the Formatting toolbar italicizes text.

1. Click on the **control** that you want to italicize. It will be selected.

2. Click on the **Italic button**.

The text will be italicized.

Underlining Text

The Underline button on the Formatting toolbar underlines text.

1. Click on the **control** that you want to underline. It will be selected.

2. Click on the **Underline button**.

The text will be underlined.

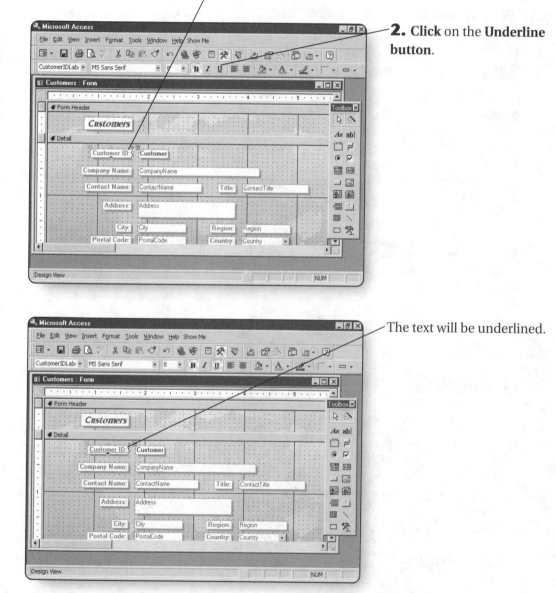

SETTING ALIGNMENT

On Access forms, you can align controls to the left or to the center.

1. **Click** on the **control** whose alignment you want to set.

2a. **Click** on the **Align Left button** to left align the text.

OR

2b. **Click** on the **Center button** to center the text.

The control is now aligned according to your choice in step 2.

15 Adding Fields, Buttons, and Boxes to Forms

In Design View, you can further customize your form by adding fields and controls such as combo boxes, list boxes, and option groups. In this chapter, you'll learn how to:

✦ Add form controls in Design View

✦ Add fields to forms

✦ Add combo and list boxes

✦ Add option groups

ADDING FORM CONTROLS IN DESIGN VIEW

After you create a form with the Form Wizard or AutoForm feature, you'll probably make minor modifications to the form's appearance. You may also want to add additional fields to the form or add controls such as list boxes, combo boxes, or option groups. To add additional controls to a form, you'll open it in Design View.

CAUTION

If you need to add more than one or two additional fields or controls, it's usually easier to create a new form. Making major form modifications takes a lot of time and can often lead to less than desirable results.

1. **Click** on the **Forms tab** in the main database window.

2. **Click** on the **form** that you want to modify. It will be selected.

3. **Click** on the **Design button**. The form will open in Design View.

NOTE

Immediately open a form in Design View by choosing the Modify the Form's Design option button on the final Form Wizard step.

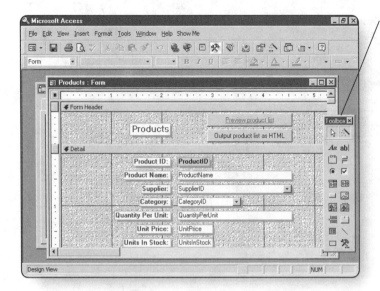

When you open a form in Design View, you'll see the Form Design Toolbox, which contains a series of buttons to help you create form controls.

The Combo Box, List Box, and Option Group buttons are examples of Toolbox buttons that create form controls. These buttons open wizards that guide you through control creation; others simply place a control directly on the form.

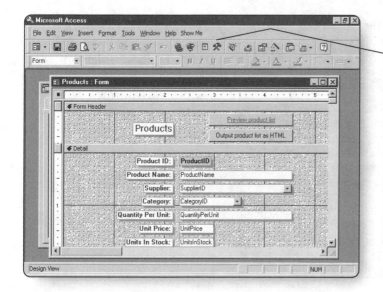

TIP

If the Toolbox doesn't appear, click on the Toolbox button.

NOTE

You can delete a field or control from a form by selecting it and pressing the Delete key.

ADDING FIELDS TO FORMS

You can add a new field control to your form through the field list, a small window that lists all the table or query fields available for use with the form.

1. Click on **View**. The View menu will appear.

2. Click on **Field List**. The field list will appear.

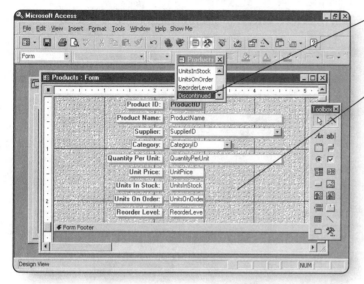

3. Click on the **field in the field list** that you want to include on your form.

4. Drag the **field** to the location on the form where you want to place it.

A control for that field will appear on the form.

NOTE

Most fields display as text box controls, but there are some exceptions. Yes/No fields display as check boxes, OLE fields display as bound object frames, and Lookup fields display as list boxes.

ADDING COMBO AND LIST BOXES

Access 97 Form Design includes wizards that help you add list boxes and combo boxes to your forms. The List Box Wizard and Combo Box Wizard are nearly identical, but each results in a different type of control.

A list box control creates a list box from which the user can select one of the listed values.

A combo box control also creates a list box of choices, but adds the flexibility of allowing the user to also type in a specific value.

You can create combo boxes or list boxes that work in three different ways. The box can:

✦ Look up values in another table or query. For example, you might want to create a control that lists all the values of the CustomerName field in a Customer table.

✦ Display a list of values that you enter. In this type of control, you enter whatever values you want and aren't limited to what already exists in a table or query.

✦ Find a record in your form that's based on the value you select in your combo or list box.

The procedure to create each of these types of combo or list boxes is somewhat similar, but to avoid confusion, I've described each procedure separately.

Creating a Combo Box or List Box That Looks Up Values

A wizard will guide you through the process of creating a combo or list box that looks up values in a specified table or query.

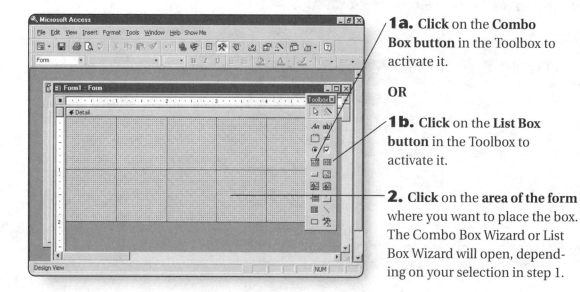

1a. **Click** on the **Combo Box button** in the Toolbox to activate it.

OR

1b. **Click** on the **List Box button** in the Toolbox to activate it.

2. **Click** on the **area of the form** where you want to place the box. The Combo Box Wizard or List Box Wizard will open, depending on your selection in step 1.

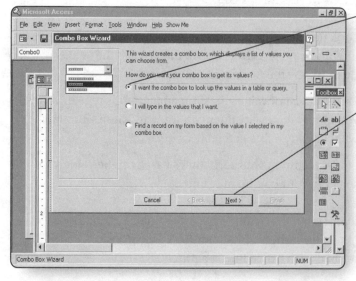

3. **Click** on the **I want the combo box (or list box) to look up the values in a table or query option button**.

4. **Click** on **Next** to continue.

Choosing a Table or Query

Next, you'll choose a table or query that contains the combo or list box values.

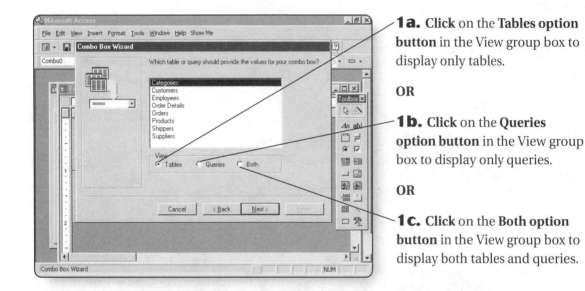

1a. **Click** on the **Tables option button** in the View group box to display only tables.

OR

1b. **Click** on the **Queries option button** in the View group box to display only queries.

OR

1c. **Click** on the **Both option button** in the View group box to display both tables and queries.

2. **Click** on the **table** or **query** which contains the values for the combo or list box.

3. **Click** on **Next** to continue.

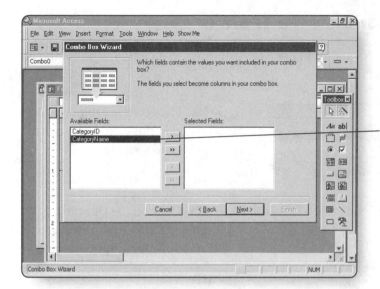

Selecting Fields

You'll select the fields to include as combo box or list box columns.

1. Choose the **first field** you want to include from the Available Fields: list.

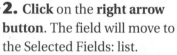

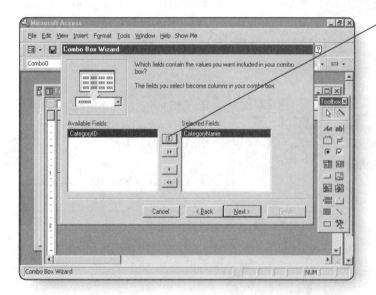

2. Click on the **right arrow button**. The field will move to the Selected Fields: list.

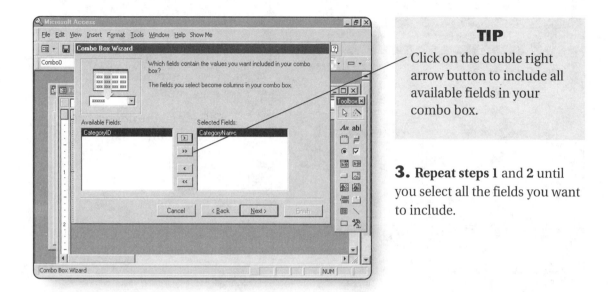

TIP

Click on the double right arrow button to include all available fields in your combo box.

3. **Repeat steps 1** and **2** until you select all the fields you want to include.

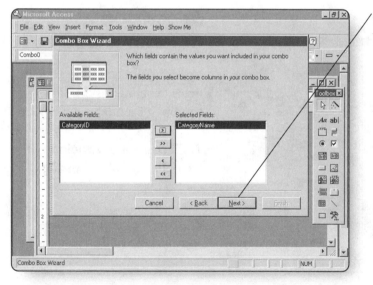

4. **Click** on **Next**. The wizard will continue to the next step.

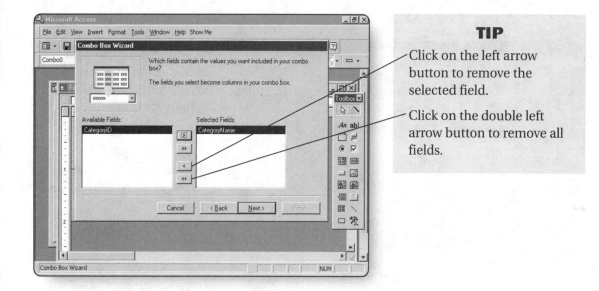

TIP

Click on the left arrow button to remove the selected field.

Click on the double left arrow button to remove all fields.

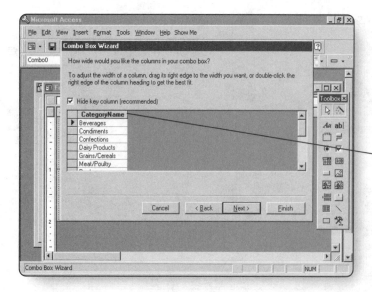

Specifying Column Width

Next, you'll specify how wide to make the columns in your combo or list box.

1. Place the **mouse pointer** on the right edge of an existing column.

2. Drag the **column** to the appropriate width.

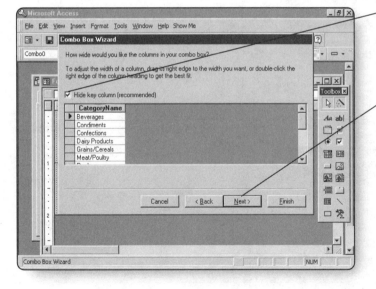

TIP

Double-click on the column's right edge to get the best fit.

3. **Click** on the **hide key column (recommended) check box** to hide the primary key column.

4. **Click** on **Next** to continue.

Determining What to Do with the Value

You can either save the combo or list box value for future use or store it in another field.

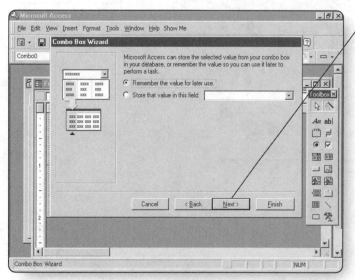

1a. **Click** on the **Remember the value for later use option button** to save the value in memory for future use.

OR

1b. **Choose** a **field** in the list box next to the Store that value in this field option button to store the combo box value.

2. **Click** on **Next** to continue.

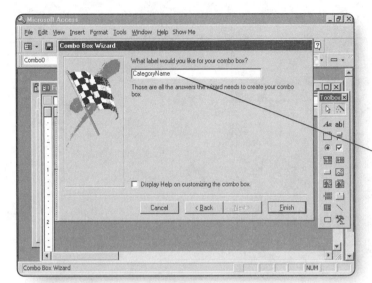

Finishing the Combo or List Box

In the final wizard step, you'll create a label for the combo or list box.

1. **Enter** a **name** for your box in the text box.

2. **Click** on the **Display Help on customizing the combo box (or list box) check box** if you want to display a help window.

3. **Click** on **Finish**.

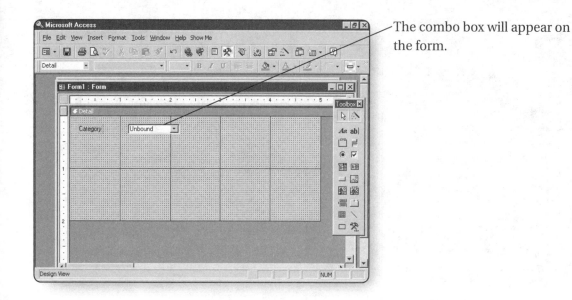

The combo box will appear on the form.

Creating a Combo or List Box in Which You Enter Values

You can also create a combo or list box in which you enter the box values directly rather than taking them from an existing report or query.

1a. **Click** on the **Combo Box button** in the Toolbox to activate it.

OR

1b. **Click** on the **List Box button** in the Toolbox to activate it.

2. **Click** on the **area of the form** where you want to place the box. The wizard will open.

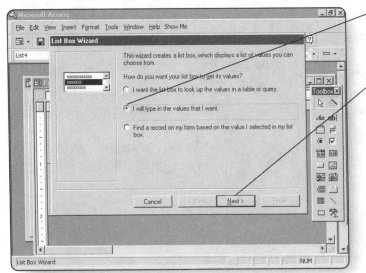

3. **Click** on the **I will type in the values that I want option button**.

4. **Click** on **Next** to continue.

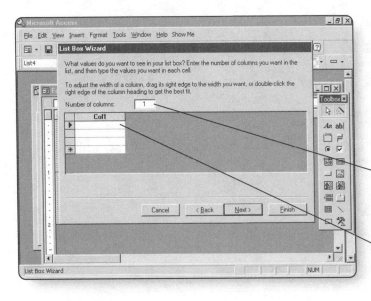

Entering the Box Values

Next, you'll enter the values that you want to appear in the combo or list box and adjust the column width.

1. **Enter** the **number of columns** you need in the Number of Columns: text box.

2. **Type** in the **values** you want to include in each column.

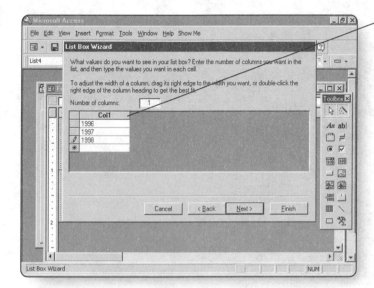

3. **Place** the **mouse pointer** on the right edge of the column you want to adjust.

4. **Drag** the **column** to the appropriate width.

5. **Repeat steps** 3 and 4 until you adjust all necessary columns.

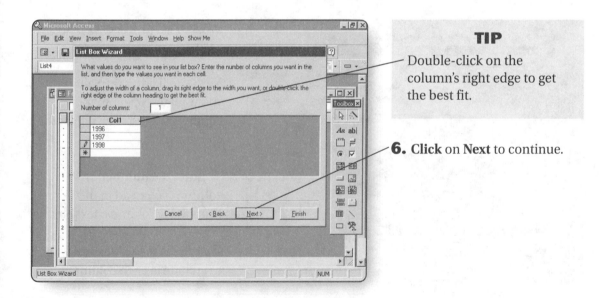

TIP

Double-click on the column's right edge to get the best fit.

6. **Click** on **Next** to continue.

Saving or Storing the Box Value

You can either save the combo or list box value for future use or store it in another field.

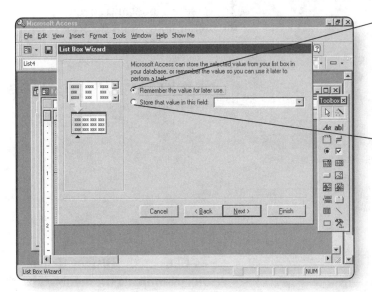

1a. Click on the **Remember the value for later use option button** to save the value in memory for future use.

OR

1b. Choose a **field** in the list box next to the Store that value in this field option button to store the box value.

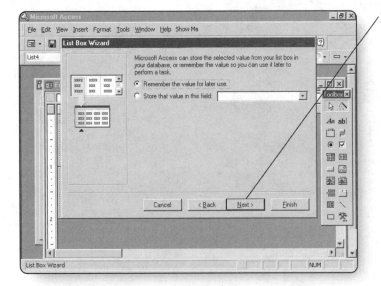

2. Click on **Next** to continue.

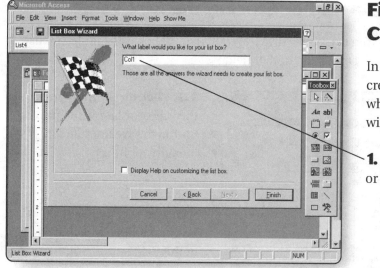

Finishing the Combo or List Box

In the final wizard step, you'll create a label and specify whether to open the help window.

1. **Enter** a **name** for your combo or list box in the text box.

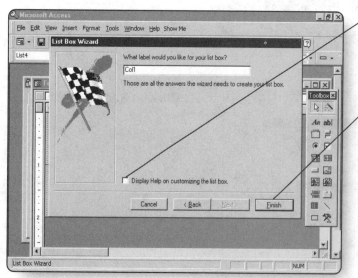

2. **Click** on the **Display Help on customizing the combo box (or list box) check box** if you want to display a help window.

3. **Click** on **Finish**.

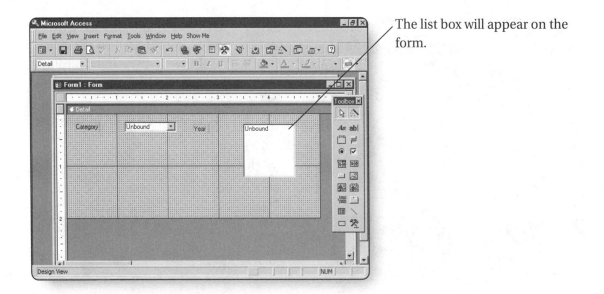

The list box will appear on the form.

Creating a Combo or List Box That Finds a Record in the Form

Finally, you can create a combo or list box that will locate a record in the current form.

1a. **Click** on the **Combo Box button** in the Toolbox to activate it.

OR

1b. **Click** on the **List Box button** in the Toolbox to activate it.

2. **Click** on the **area of the form** where you want to place the combo or list box. The wizard will open.

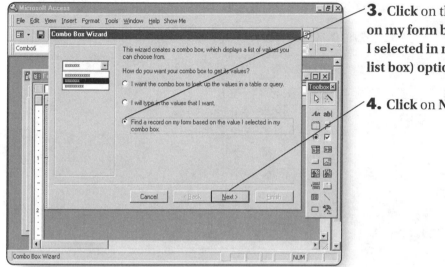

3. **Click** on the **Find a record on my form based on the value I selected in my combo box (or list box)** option button.

4. **Click** on **Next** to continue.

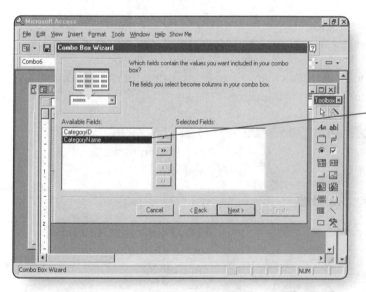

Selecting Fields

Next, you'll select the fields to include.

1. **Choose** the **first field** you want to include from the Available Fields: list.

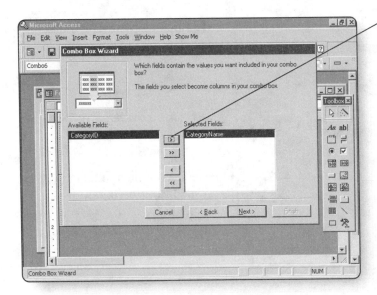

2. Click on the **right arrow button**. The field will move to the Selected Fields: list.

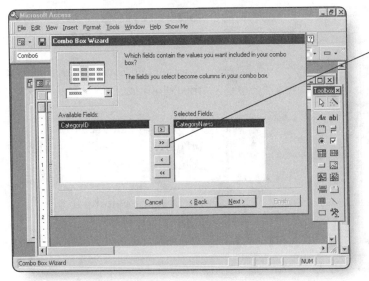

TIP

Click on the double right arrow button to include all available fields in your box.

3. Repeat steps 1 and **2** until you select all the fields you want to include in your combo box.

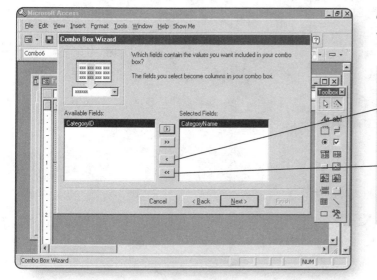

4. **Click** on **Next**. The wizard will continue to the next step.

TIP

Click on the left arrow button to remove the selected field.

Click on the double left arrow button to remove all fields.

Specifying Column Width

Now specify how wide to make the columns.

1. **Place** the **mouse pointer** on the right edge of an existing column.

2. **Drag** the **column** to the appropriate width.

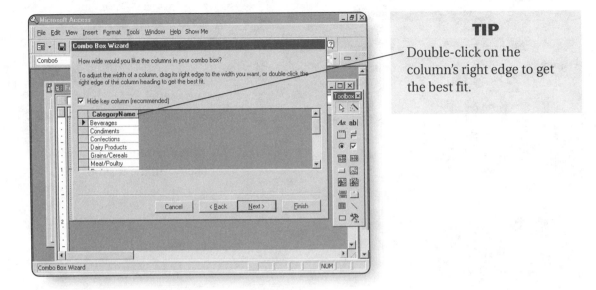

TIP
Double-click on the
column's right edge to get
the best fit.

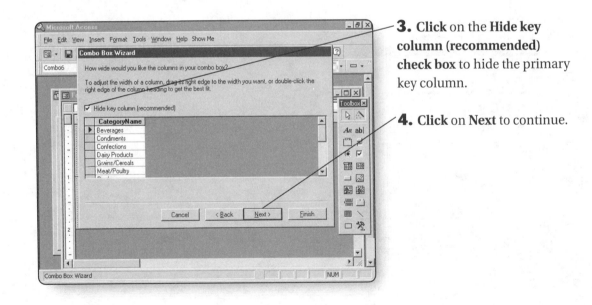

3. **Click** on the **Hide key
column (recommended)
check box** to hide the primary
key column.

4. **Click** on **Next** to continue.

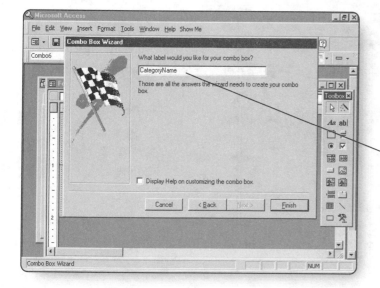

Finishing the Combo or Box

In the final wizard step, you'll create a label for the box and specify help options.

1. **Enter** a **name** for your combo or list box in the text box.

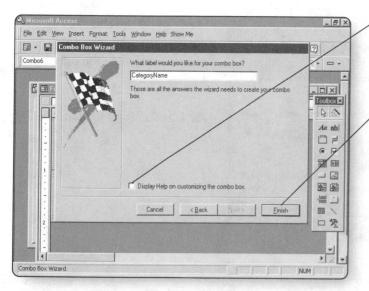

2. **Click** on the **Display Help on customizing the combo box (or list box) check box** if you want to display a help window.

3. **Click** on **Finish**.

ADDING OPTION GROUPS

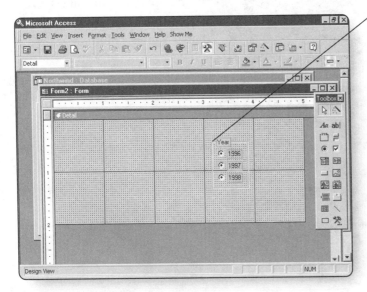

Another type of control you can add to a form is an option group. An option group lets a user choose one of several displayed options. The options are usually preceded by option buttons, but you can also use check boxes or toggles. You enter the actual options as label names for the option group.

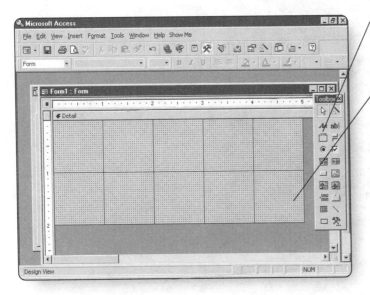

1. Click on the **Option Group button** in the Toolbox to activate it.

2. Click on the **area of the form** where you want to place the box. The Option Group Wizard will open.

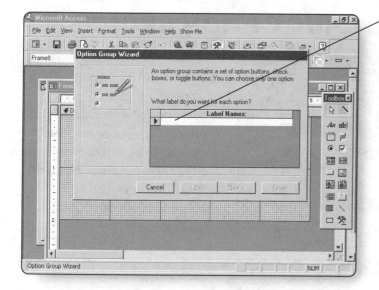

3. Type in the **label name** for each option button you want to display in the group box in the Label Names: column.

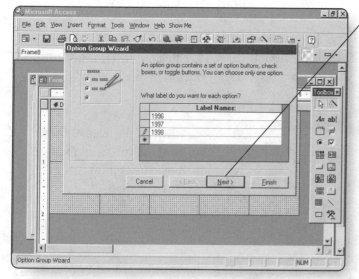

4. **Click** on **Next** to continue.

Specifying a Default Choice

You can indicate a default option that will display for every record, but it isn't required.

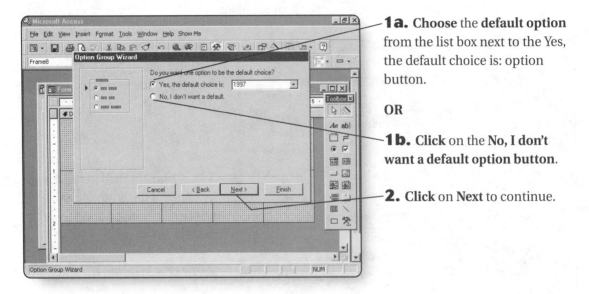

1a. Choose the **default option** from the list box next to the Yes, the default choice is: option button.

OR

1b. Click on the **No, I don't want a default option button**.

2. Click on **Next** to continue.

Setting Option Values

You assign a numeric value to each option in an option group. Access then saves this numeric value for later use or stores it in a table. The default numeric value series is 1, 2, 3, and so on.

1. Enter the **option value** for each label name in the Values: column.

2. Click on **Next**. The wizard will continue to the next step.

Saving or Storing the Option Group Value

You can either save the option group value for future use or store it in another form field.

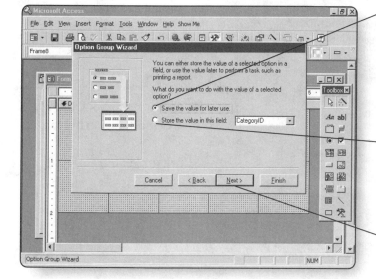

1a. **Click** on the **Save the value for later use option button** to save the value in memory for future use.

OR

1b. **Choose** a **field** in the list box next to the Store the value in this field option button in which to store the value.

2. **Click** on **Next** to continue.

Specifying Controls and Styles

You can display your options as option buttons, check boxes, or toggle buttons. You can also choose one of five different box styles.

1a. **Click** on the **Option buttons option button**.

OR

1b. Click on the **Check boxes check box**.

OR

1c. Click on the **Toggle buttons toggle button**.

2. Click on the **option button** of the style you prefer.

3. Click on **Next** to continue to the final step.

Finishing the Option Group

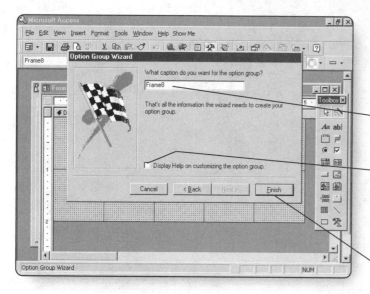

In the final step of the Option Group Wizard, you'll create a label for the option group and specify help options.

1. Enter a **name** for your option group in the text box.

2. Click on the **Display Help on customizing the option group check box** if you want to display a help window.

3. Click on **Finish**.

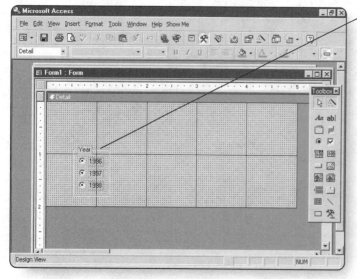

The option group will display on the form.

16 Entering Data in a Form

Forms offer an alternative way to enter data in Access tables. Using a form, you can enter data from a more visual perspective. You can also enter data in more than one table. In this chapter, you'll learn how to:

✦ Open a form in Form View

✦ Use edit mode to enter form data

✦ Use data entry mode to enter form data

✦ Save form data entries

OPENING A FORM IN FORM VIEW

To enter data in a form, you need to open it in Form View.

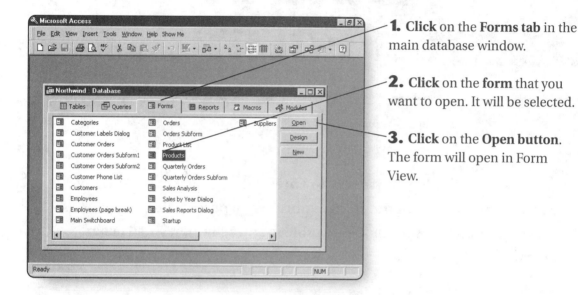

1. Click on the **Forms tab** in the main database window.

2. Click on the **form** that you want to open. It will be selected.

3. Click on the **Open button**. The form will open in Form View.

Form View offers an alternative, more visual way to enter data into a table or tables. You enter data in forms through a number of form controls. The most common form controls you'll use to enter data include the following:

✦ **Text box**. Type an entry in the box.

✦ **Check box**. Click on the check box to select the field. Choose an entry from the drop-down list or type your own entry.

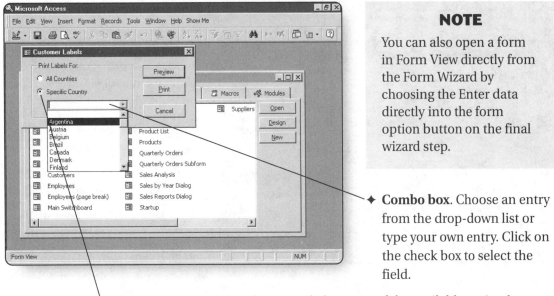

You can also open a form in Form View directly from the Form Wizard by choosing the Enter data directly into the form option button on the final wizard step.

✦ **Combo box**. Choose an entry from the drop-down list or type your own entry. Click on the check box to select the field.

✦ **Option button**. Click on one of the available option buttons in an option group box.

NAVIGATING IN FORM VIEW

The current form record number displays in the record number box at the bottom of the screen. Several navigation buttons surround this box. These help you navigate the form. Using these buttons, you can move to the first, preceding, next, or last form record.

You can also use the mouse to navigate the form or select the field you want. In addition, Access also provides several other form navigation commands:

Enter or Tab   Navigates to the next field.

Shift+Tab   Navigates to the preceding field.

Page Up   Navigates up one screen.

Page Down   Navigates down one screen.

USING EDIT MODE TO ENTER DATA IN A FORM

One way to enter data in a form is to use *Edit mode*, which creates a blank form after the last complete form record.

1. **Click** on the **New Record button**. A blank form record will appear.

2. **Enter data** in the new form.

3. **Repeat steps 1** and **2** until you finish adding data.

TIP

You can also click on the New Record button to the right of the navigation buttons to add a new record.

NOTE

Access automatically enters the next consecutive number in an AutoNumber field.

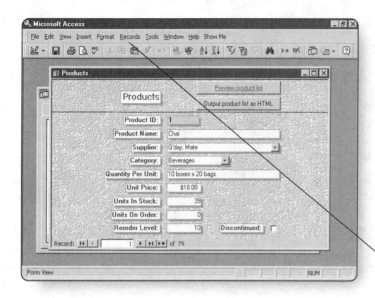

USING DATA ENTRY MODE TO ENTER DATA IN FORMS

Data Entry mode is another way to enter data in a form. Data Entry mode displays a blank form and temporarily hides all existing form records from view.

1. **Click** on **Records**. The Records menu will appear.

2. **Click** on **Data Entry**. Data Entry mode will be activated.

3. Enter data in the new blank form.

4. Click on the **New Record button** to open another blank form.

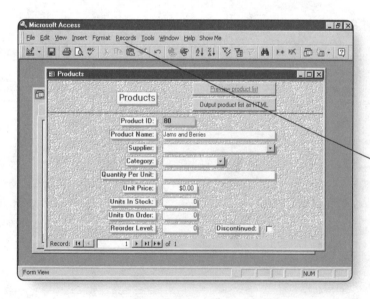

5. **Enter data** in this form.

6. **Repeat steps 4** and **5** until you finish entering data.

Exiting Data Entry Mode

You can deactivate Data Entry mode when you finish data entry.

1. **Click** on **Records**. The Records menu will appear.

2. Click on **Remove Filter/Sort**.

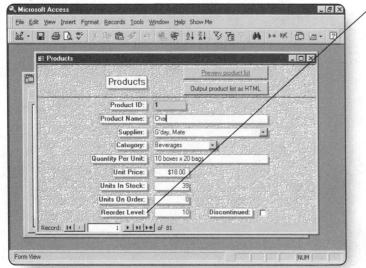

The hidden form records will appear again.

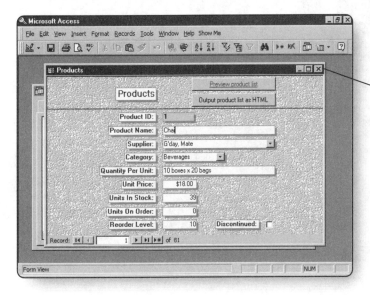

SAVING FORM DATA ENTRIES

To exit a form and save your entries, click on the Close button.

PART V REVIEW QUESTIONS

1. How do you automatically create a form in a vertical format? *Head down to "Creating a Columnar AutoForm" in Chapter 12*

2. What automated feature lets you create a form that displays your table data in rows and columns? *Scroll over to "Creating a Tabular AutoForm" in Chapter 12*

3. How can you get assistance in creating a form in which you choose fields and format? *Jump to "Starting the Form Wizard" in Chapter 13*

4. Where do you set the overall appearance of your form in the Form Wizard? *Flip to "Choosing a Form Style" in Chapter 13*

5. In which view do you open a form when you want to modify its appearance? *Look at "Opening a Form in Design View" in Chapter 14*

6. How do you change a form's AutoFormat? *Go to "Selecting Specific Formatting Options" in Chapter 14*

7. Where can you add form controls? *See "Adding Form Controls in Design View" in Chapter 15*

8. How can you add drop-down lists to your form? *Jump to "Adding Combo and List Boxes" in Chapter 15*

9. How do you enter data in a form? *Turn to "Opening a Form in Form View" in Chapter 16*

10. Which mode temporarily hides all existing records from view while you enter data in a form? *Find out in "Using Data Entry Mode to Enter Data in Forms" in Chapter 16*

PART VI

Querying for Information

roduc

ducts

roduct ID:

duct Name:

Supplier:

Category:

uantity Per Unit:

Unit Price:

Units In Stock:

Units On Order:

17 Using the Simple Query Wizard

The Simple Query Wizard guides you through the creation of a basic select query that extracts specific fields from tables or other queries. In this chapter, you'll learn how to:

✦ Start the Simple Query Wizard

✦ Select fields

✦ Choose a detail or summary query

✦ Finish the query

STARTING THE SIMPLE QUERY WIZARD

The Simple Query Wizard helps you to create a simple select query from fields you specify. In Access 97, a *select query* selects data you choose from single or multiple tables or queries. For example, you could create a query that lists only certain fields in a table containing a large number of fields.

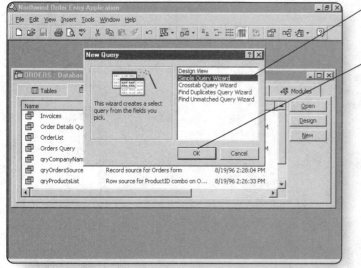

1. Click on the **Queries tab** in the main database window.

2. Click on **New**. The New Query dialog box will open.

3. Click on the **Simple Query Wizard option**.

4. Click on **OK**. The Simple Query Wizard will open.

NOTE

A *query* is a way to extract information from your database. In Access 97, you can create queries to select, analyze, and summarize specific data.

SELECTING FIELDS

In the next step, you choose the specific fields to include in your query and indicate the table or other query in which they are located.

1. **Click** on the **table or query** from which you want to select your query field in the Tables/Queries: drop-down list. A list of the fields for that table/query will appear.

2. **Choose** the **first field** you want to include in your query from the Available Fields: list.

3. **Click** on the **right arrow button**. The field will move to the Selected Fields: list.

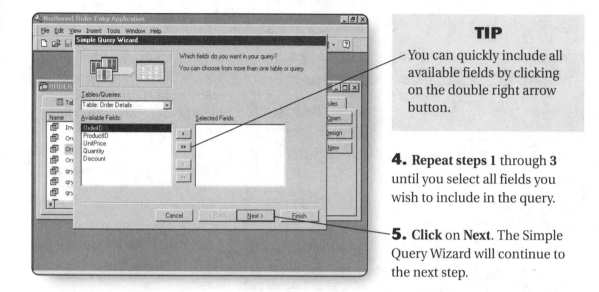

You can quickly include all available fields by clicking on the double right arrow button.

4. **Repeat steps 1** through **3** until you select all fields you wish to include in the query.

5. **Click** on **Next**. The Simple Query Wizard will continue to the next step.

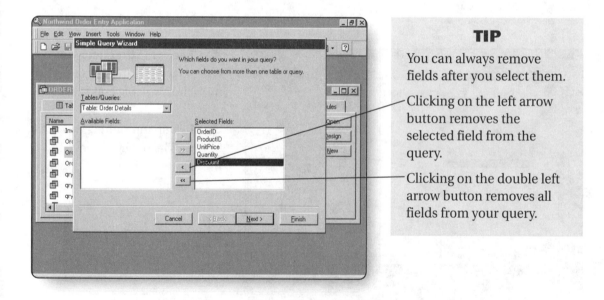

You can always remove fields after you select them.

Clicking on the left arrow button removes the selected field from the query.

Clicking on the double left arrow button removes all fields from your query.

CHOOSING A DETAIL OR SUMMARY QUERY

If you include number fields in your query, you can display either detailed or summary information.

Creating a Detail Query

A detail query will include all fields in all records.

1. Click on the **Detail option button**.

2. Click on **Next** to continue to the last step where you will finish your query.

CAUTION

This step will not appear if your query doesn't include any numeric fields.

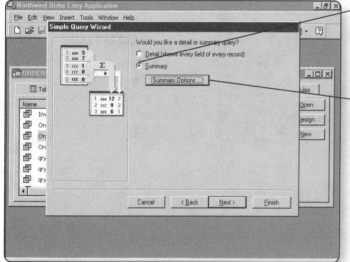

Creating a Summary Query

A summary query lets you summarize information in your select query. Through the Summary Options dialog box, you can specify up to four different summary options for each numeric field in your query. These options include the ability to summarize a field as well as to display its average, minimum, or maximum.

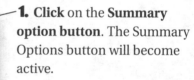

1. **Click** on the **Summary option button**. The Summary Options button will become active.

2. **Click** on the **Summary Options button**. The Summary Options dialog box will open.

3. **Click** on the **check box** for each field and summary option combination to include in your query.

4. **Click** on the **Count records in Order Details check box** to display a record count in the query.

5. **Click** on **OK** to return to the Simple Query Wizard.

6. Click on **Next** to continue to the next step to finish the query.

FINISHING THE QUERY

In the Simple Query Wizard's last step, you enter a query title and determine how to open the query.

1. Enter a **name** for the query in the text box.

2a. Click on the **Open the query to view information option button** to open the query in Datasheet View.

OR

2b. Click on the **Modify the query design option button** to open the query in Design View.

3. Click on the **Display Help on working with the query check box** to display the help window when you open the query.

4. Click on **Finish**. The query will open based on your selection in step 2.

If you choose to open the query in this final wizard step, the query displays the fields you selected in Datasheet View.

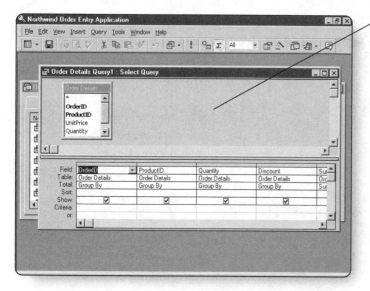

If you choose to modify the query's design in this step, it opens in Design View, where you can modify and customize the query.

18 Using the Crosstab Query Wizard

The Crosstab Query Wizard helps you build a crosstab query that analyzes data in a spreadsheet format. In this chapter, you'll learn how to:

✦ Start the Crosstab Query Wizard

✦ Select a table

✦ Select fields

✦ Select a column heading

✦ Select a summary method

✦ Finish the query

STARTING THE CROSSTAB QUERY WIZARD

Using the Crosstab Query Wizard, you can summarize information in a spreadsheet format. Crosstab queries crosstabulate information and let you look at your table data in different ways.

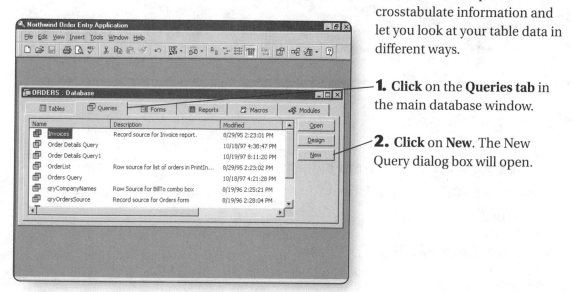

1. **Click** on the **Queries tab** in the main database window.

2. **Click** on **New**. The New Query dialog box will open.

3. **Click** on the **Crosstab Query Wizard option**.

4. **Click** on **OK**. The Crosstab Query Wizard will open.

NOTE

If you're new to the concept of crosstab queries, it's a good idea to write your query format on paper before using the wizard. Remember, a crosstab query looks like a spreadsheet.

SELECTING A TABLE OR QUERY

You can base your crosstab query on either a table or another query.

1a. **Click** on the **Tables option button** to view only tables.

OR

1b. **Click** on the **Queries option button** to view only queries.

OR

1c. **Click** on the **Both option button** to view both tables and queries.

2. **Click** on the **table or query** on which you want to base your crosstab query.

3. **Click** on **Next**.

SELECTING ROW HEADING FIELDS

In a crosstab query, you can select up to three fields to be the row headings—just as in a spreadsheet. The order in which you select these fields is the order in which they are sorted.

1. **Choose** the **first field** you want to include as a row heading from the Available Fields: scroll box.

2. **Click** on the **right arrow button**. The field will move to the Selected Fields: scroll box.

NOTE

The sample preview box illustrates how your crosstab query will actually look.

3. **Repeat steps 1** through **2** until you select all the fields you want to include as row headings in the query.

4. **Click** on **Next**. The wizard will continue to the next step.

TIP

It's easy to remove fields after you select them. Click on the left arrow button to remove the selected field from the query or click on the double left arrow button to remove all fields from your query.

SELECTING A COLUMN HEADING

Next, you'll select one field to be the column heading in the crosstab query.

1. Choose the **field** to be the column heading.

2. Click on **Next** to continue to the next step.

SELECTING A SUMMARY METHOD

Next, you'll select a field to summarize and the method by which to summarize it. Summary options include:

✦ Average

✦ Count

✦ First

✦ Last

✦ Maximum

✦ Minimum

✦ Standard Deviation

✦ Summary

✦ Variance

1. Choose the **field to summarize** from the Fields: list.

2. Choose the **summary method** from the Functions: list.

NOTE

Only numeric fields will display in the Fields: list because only numeric fields can be summarized.

3. Click on the **Yes, include row sums check box** if you want to summarize each row.

4. Click on **Next** to continue.

FINISHING THE QUERY

You'll enter a query title and determine how to open the query in this last step.

1. Enter a **name** for the query in the text box.

2a. Click on the **View the query option button** to open the query in Datasheet View.

OR

2b. Click on the **Modify the design option button** to open the query in Design View.

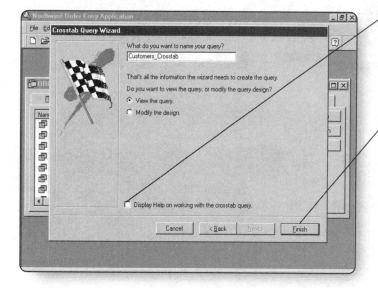

3. Click on the **Display Help on working with the crosstab query check box** if you want to have help when you open the query.

4. Click on **Finish**. The crosstab query will open based on your choice in step 2.

If you choose to view the query in this final wizard step, you'll see the end results of the crosstab query, which crosstabulates your data into a spreadsheet format.

If you choose to modify and customize the query's design in this step, you can do so.

19

Creating Queries in Design View

If you want more flexibility than a query wizard provides, you can create a query by scratch in Design View. In this chapter, you'll learn how to:

✦ Start a query in Design View

✦ Select a table

✦ Add fields

✦ Specify criteria

✦ Specify calculations

✦ View query results

✦ Save a query

STARTING A QUERY IN DESIGN VIEW

To create a query from scratch, you need to start it in Design View.

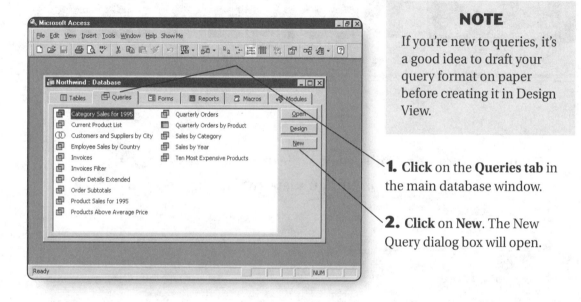

NOTE

If you're new to queries, it's a good idea to draft your query format on paper before creating it in Design View.

1. **Click** on the **Queries tab** in the main database window.

2. **Click** on **New**. The New Query dialog box will open.

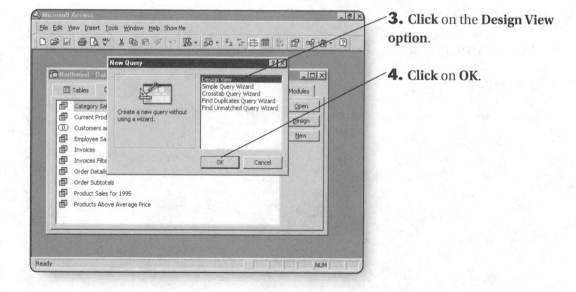

3. **Click** on the **Design View option**.

4. **Click** on **OK**.

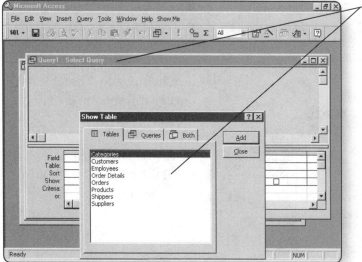

The Select Query window and Show Table dialog box will open.

SELECTING A TABLE OR QUERY

You can include fields from other tables or queries in your new query by selecting them in the Show Table dialog box.

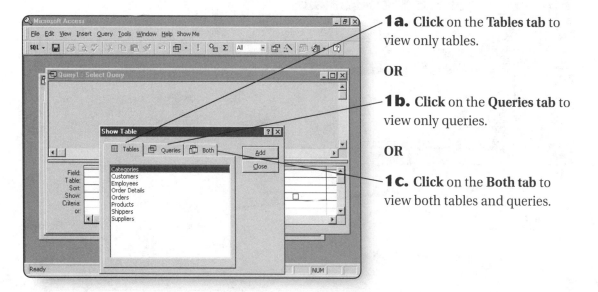

1a. Click on the **Tables tab** to view only tables.

OR

1b. Click on the **Queries tab** to view only queries.

OR

1c. Click on the **Both tab** to view both tables and queries.

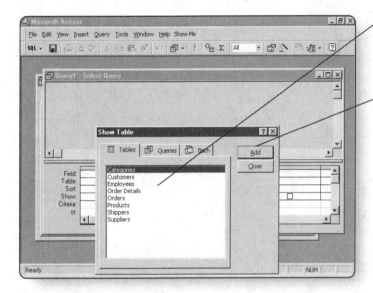

2. Click on the **table or query** you want to include in your new query.

3. Click on **Add**. The table or query will display in the Select Query window.

4. Repeat steps 2 and 3 until you finish adding the required tables and queries.

5. Click on the **Close button**. The Show Table dialog box will close.

TIP

To reopen the Show Table dialog box, click on the Show Table button in the toolbar.

The top portion of the Select Query window displays each selected table or query as a list box joined by a line. These *join lines* link *key fields*—fields that share the same field name and type. The join lines indicate table relationships that relate the data in one table to the data in another. Each selected table or query displays a list of fields that you can add to the query.

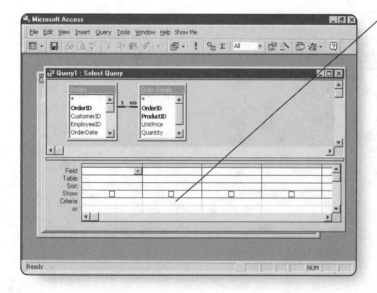

TIP

To link key fields manually, click on a field in one list box and drag it to the other linking field in another list box.

The bottom portion of the Select Query window displays the *design grid*. You'll add fields to the query by dragging them from the field lists to the design grid. The design grid is similar to a spreadsheet, with columns representing each field in the query.

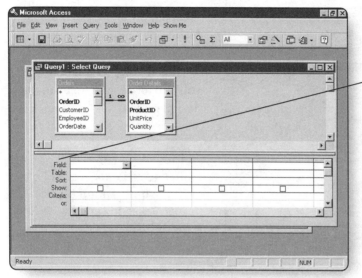

ADDING FIELDS

To add fields to your query, you'll drag them to the design grid. Once you place a field in the design grid, the Field: row will display the field name, the Table: row will display the original table, and the Show: row will display a ✔. All fields with a ✔ in the Show: row will display in your query.

TIP

Remove the ✔ from the Show: check box to temporarily hide the field from the query results.

1. Click on the **first field** you want to include in your query from the list box.

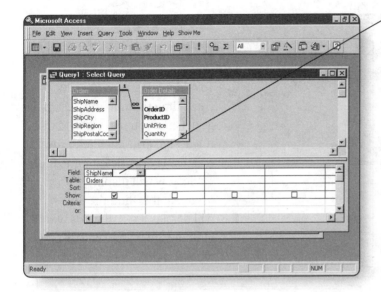

2. **Drag** the **selected field** to a Field: row in the design grid.

3. **Repeat steps 1** and **2** until you add all desired fields to the design grid.

TIP

To add all fields in a list box to the query, double-click on the list box and drag it to the design grid.

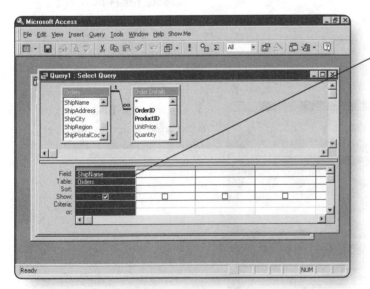

Deleting Fields

If you want to delete a field from the design grid, click on the field selector for that field and then press the Delete key on your keyboard.

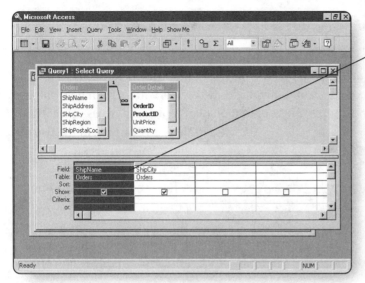

Moving Fields

To move a field on the design grid, click on the field selector for that field. The field column will be highlighted. Drag it to the new location.

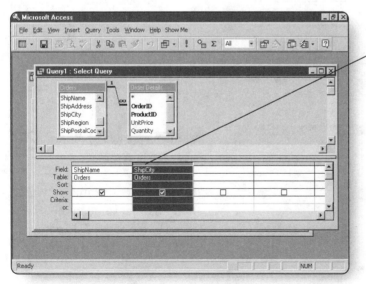

Inserting Fields

To insert a field between two existing fields in the design grid, drag the new field to the column location where you want to insert it.

SPECIFYING CRITERIA

Once you've selected all your query fields, you can narrow your query to include only data that matches specific criteria. You may want to display only records with certain field values, for example. A query that displays only employees in a certain state is an example of the use of criteria. You can also use wildcard patterns in your criteria or indicate what values *not* to include.

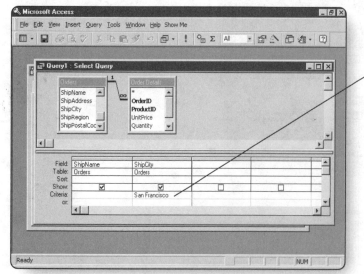

You specify query criteria in the Criteria: row in the design grid.

Specifying Exact Matches

To specify an exact match, you'll enter an exact value in the Criteria: row of the field column in which you want to search.

Specifying Wildcard Patterns

Wildcards offer a way of setting criteria based on patterns or partial words rather than exact matches.

The most common wildcard operators include:

? Replaces a single character

* Replaces a number of characters

Replaces a single digit

For example, the criterion A* in a First Name field would include any first name beginning with the letter A, such as Anne, Al, or Adam. The criterion A? would only include the name Al, not Anne nor Adam.

To specify a wildcard pattern, enter the pattern in the Criteria: row of the field column in which you want to search.

Specifying Eliminations

Sometimes you want to tell the query what *not* to display, rather than what to display. For example, you might want to view all employees who are *not* residents of the USA. To specify eliminations, enter "Not" followed by the elimination term, such as "Not USA."

Specifying Dates

You can also specify dates in the Criteria: row.

You can enter an exact date, such as 1/1/98, or you can use wildcard operators to specify an entire year. For example, */*/97 would find all dates in the year 1997.

To specify more exact dates, you can use the Between . . . and operator. For example, Between 1/1/98 and 3/31/98 would find all entries between these two dates.

SORTING QUERY FIELDS

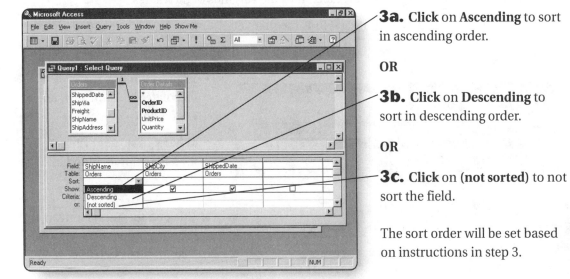

By default, query fields are not sorted. You can, however, sort any fields in either ascending or descending order.

1. Click on the **Sort: row** in the field column you want to sort. A down arrow (▼) will appear to the right of the field.

2. Click on the **down arrow** (▼). A list of options will appear.

3a. Click on **Ascending** to sort in ascending order.

OR

3b. Click on **Descending** to sort in descending order.

OR

3c. Click on **(not sorted)** to not sort the field.

The sort order will be set based on instructions in step 3.

SPECIFYING CALCULATIONS

Using a query is a convenient way to perform a calculation on a group of records. For example, you may want to know how many orders each salesperson placed last month or the total dollar amount for these orders. You'll use the Total: row in the design grid to specify calculation criteria. In Access 97, you can specify the following calculation types:

✦ **Group By**. Identifies the group to calculate.

✦ **Sum**. Totals the values.

✦ **Avg**. Averages the values.

✦ **Min**. Finds the minimum value.

✦ **Max**. Finds the maximum value.

✦ **Count**. Counts the number of values.

✦ **StDev**. Calculates the standard deviation of the values.

✦ **Var**. Calculates the variance of the values.

✦ **First**. Finds the first field values.

✦ **Last**. Finds the last field values.

✦ **Expression**. Creates a calculated field through an expression.

✦ **Where**. Indicates criteria for a field not included in the query.

1. Click on the **Totals button** on the Toolbar. The Total: row will appear in the design grid.

2. Click on the **Total: row** for the first field whose calculation type you want to specify.

3. Click on the **down arrow (▼)** to the right of the field. A list of calculation types will appear.

4. Click on the **calculation type** you want to apply to that field.

5. Repeat steps 2 through **4** until you specify a calculation type for each field in the query.

VIEWING QUERY RESULTS

Click on the Run button to view the query results.

The query displays in Datasheet View. If the results aren't as you intended, you can return to Design View to make further modifications.

To return to Design View, click on the View button.

SAVING A QUERY

Once you finish your query and verify the results are what you want, you can save it.

1. Click on the **Save button**. The Save As dialog box will open.

2. Enter a **name for the query** in the Query Name: text box.

3. Click on OK.

The query will be saved.

PART VI REVIEW QUESTIONS

1. Which wizard helps you create a basic select query? *Choose "Starting the Simple Query Wizard" in Chapter 17*

2. What options does a summary query offer? *Take your pick in "Creating a Summary Query" in Chapter 17*

3. What are the two ways you can open a finished query? *Find out in "Finishing the Query" in Chapter 17*

4. How do you create a query that summarizes information in a spreadsheet format? *Learn in "Starting the Crosstab Query Wizard" in Chapter 18*

5. How many fields can you select as row headings in a crosstab query? *Count them in "Selecting Row Heading Fields" in Chapter 18*

6. How many different summary methods do crosstab queries provide? *Turn to "Selecting a Summary Method" in Chapter 18*

7. In which view can you create a query from scratch? *See "Starting a Query in Design View" in Chapter 19*

8. How do you use the design grid in creating a query? *Map it out in "Selecting a Table or Query" in Chapter 19*

9. How can you narrow your query to include or exclude specific information? *Skim over "Specifying Criteria" in Chapter 19*

10. Where can you set calculation criteria in a query? *Place your bet on "Specifying Calculations" in Chapter 19*

PART VII

Working with Reports

rod
duct
roduct ID
duct Name
Supplie
Category
uantity Per Uni
Unit Price
Units In Stock
Units On Orde

20 Creating an AutoReport

You can simply and easily create basic reports in Access 97 using the AutoReport feature. Using AutoReport, you can automatically create both columnar and tabular reports that you base on a selected table or query. In this chapter, you'll learn how to:

✦ Create a Columnar AutoReport

✦ Create a Tabular AutoReport

✦ Save and close a report

CREATING A COLUMNAR AUTOREPORT

You can automatically create a columnar report based on a selected table or query using the AutoReport feature. In a columnar report, one record at a time will appear on the page, in a vertical format. A columnar report follows the same format as a columnar form.

1. Click on the **Reports tab** in the main database window.

2. Click on **New**. The New Report dialog box will open.

3. Click on the **AutoReport: Columnar option**.

4. Click on the **down arrow** (▼) next to the list box. A list of choices will appear.

5. Click on the **table** on which you want to base your report.

6. Click on **OK**.

A columnar report based on this table will appear in Print Preview. You can print this report as is or modify its design.

Orders

Order ID	10330
Customer	LILA-Supermercado
Employee	Leverling, Janet
Order Date	16-Nov-94
Required Date	14-Dec-94
Shipped Date	28-Nov-94
Ship Via	Speedy Express
Freight	$12.75
Ship Name	LILA-Supermercado

NOTE

A report that you create using AutoReport has several defaults. It includes all fields in the table or query on which it's based. It defaults to the Casual report style and it automatically displays in portrait orientation. If you don't want these defaults, you can later modify the report design or you can use the Report Wizard to create your report.

CREATING A TABULAR AUTOREPORT

Using the AutoReport feature, you can also create a tabular report based on a selected table or query. A tabular report displays your table data in a row and column format. Tabular reports are very similar to tabular forms.

1. Click on the **Reports tab** in the main database window.

2. Click on **New**. The New Report dialog box will open.

3. **Click** on the **AutoReport: Tabular option**.

4. **Click** on the **down arrow** (▼) next to the list box. A list of choices will appear.

5. **Click** on the **desired table**.

6. **Click** on **OK**.

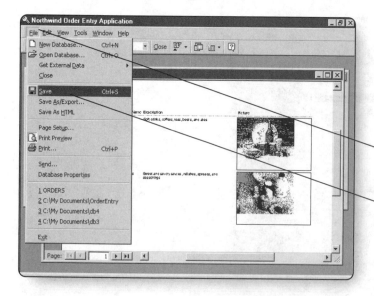

A tabular report based on this table will appear in Print Preview.

SAVING A REPORT

After you create a report, you'll want to save it.

1. Click on **File**. The File menu will appear.

2. Click on **Save**. The Save As dialog box will open.

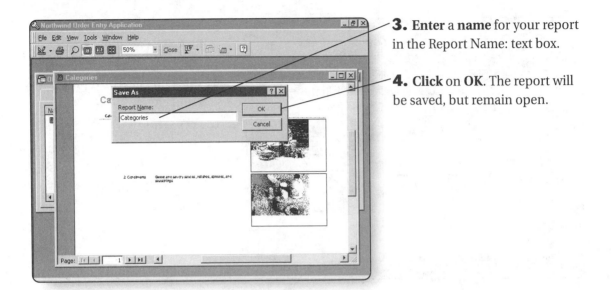

3. **Enter** a **name** for your report in the Report Name: text box.

4. **Click** on **OK**. The report will be saved, but remain open.

Saving and Closing a Report

You can also save and close a report simultaneously.

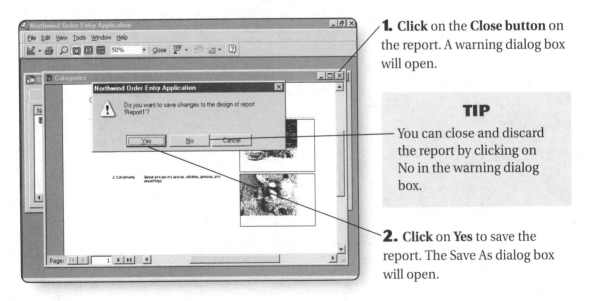

1. **Click** on the **Close button** on the report. A warning dialog box will open.

TIP

You can close and discard the report by clicking on No in the warning dialog box.

2. **Click** on **Yes** to save the report. The Save As dialog box will open.

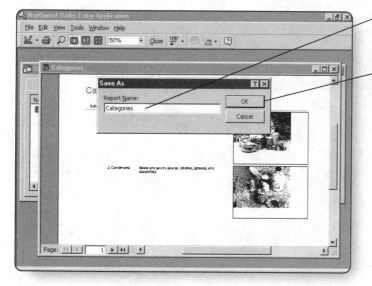

3. **Enter** a **name** for your report in the Report Name: text box.

4. **Click** on **OK**. The report will save and close.

21 Creating a Report with the Report Wizard

Using the Access 97 Report Wizard, you can create a report in a matter of minutes and still have the opportunity to specify many of your own parameters. The Report Wizard lets you set grouping, sorting, and summary options as well as choose your own styles and layouts. In this chapter, you'll learn how to:

✦ Start the Report Wizard

✦ Select fields

✦ Create groupings and sort orders

✦ Specify summary options

✦ Specify the report layout and style

✦ Finish the report

STARTING THE REPORT WIZARD

The Report Wizard offers step-by-step guidance on creating detailed reports, including those that contain fields from more than one table or query.

1. Click on the **Reports tab** in the main database window.

2. Click on **New**. The New Report dialog box will open.

3. Click on the **Report Wizard option**.

4. Click on **OK**. The Report Wizard will open.

SELECTING FIELDS

In the second step, you choose the specific fields for your report, including the table or query in which they are located.

1. **Click** on the **table or query** from which you want to select your report field in the Tables/Queries: drop-down list. A list of the fields for that table/query will appear.

2. **Choose** the **first field** you want to include in your report from the Available Fields: list.

3. **Click** on the **right arrow button**. The field will move to the Selected Fields: scroll box.

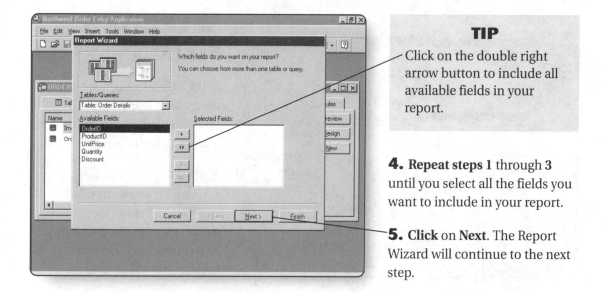

Click on the double right arrow button to include all available fields in your report.

4. Repeat steps 1 through **3** until you select all the fields you want to include in your report.

5. Click on **Next**. The Report Wizard will continue to the next step.

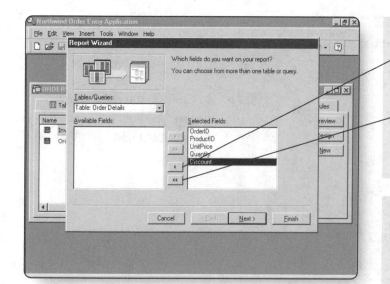

Click on the left arrow button to remove the selected field from the report.

Click on the double left arrow button to remove all fields from your report.

Remember that a report can only contain a certain number of fields on one page. Consider carefully the exact information you need to include, as well as the width of each field, when designing a report.

CREATING GROUPINGS

In Access 97, you can create report groupings based on one or several fields.

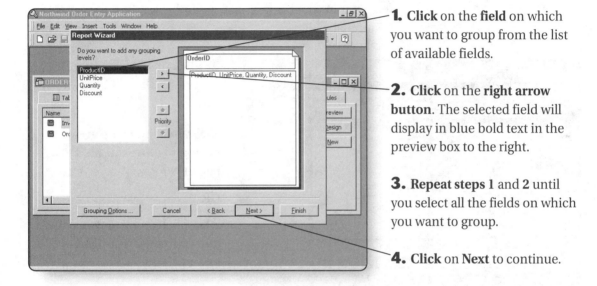

1. Click on the **field** on which you want to group from the list of available fields.

2. Click on the **right arrow button**. The selected field will display in blue bold text in the preview box to the right.

3. Repeat steps 1 and **2** until you select all the fields on which you want to group.

4. Click on **Next** to continue.

TIP

To remove a field grouping, click on the field name.

Then click on the left arrow button.

Changing the Grouping Priority

In the preview window, the grouping level fields display in blue bold text and are listed in order of grouping priority, with each subsequent level slightly indented. The order is based on the order in which you specify grouping levels, but you can easily change it.

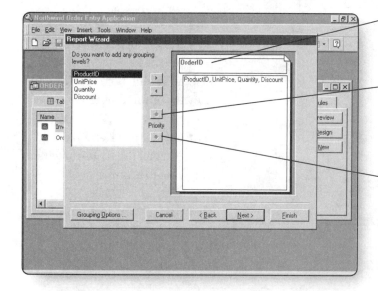

1. **Click** on the **grouping field** in the preview box whose priority you want to change.

2a. **Click** on the **up arrow button** to move this field to a higher priority.

OR

2b. **Click** on the **down arrow button** to move this field to a lower priority.

3. **Repeat steps 1** and **2** until you've changed the grouping priorities to the desired order.

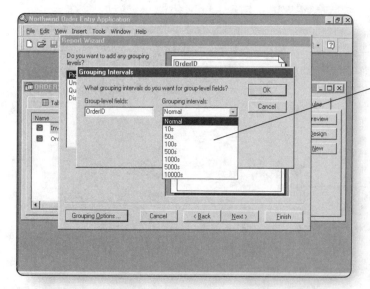

Setting Grouping Intervals

Access also offers the option of grouping by specified intervals. Depending on the data type of the field, the available grouping interval options will vary. For example, number fields include grouping options in several different multiples, and text fields include grouping options based on initial letters.

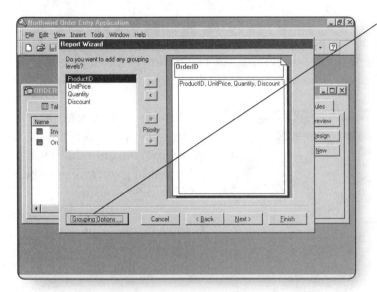

1. Click on the **Grouping Options button**. The Grouping Intervals dialog box will open.

2. Choose the **desired interval** from the Grouping intervals: drop-down list.

3. Repeat step 2 until you have set all grouping intervals.

4. Click on **OK**.

NOTE

Grouping intervals are only available for fields on which you've already specified a grouping level.

SPECIFYING A SORT ORDER

Using the Report Wizard, you can sort up to four different fields in either ascending (the default) or descending order.

1. **Click** on the **first field** on which you want to sort your report from the drop-down list. The ascending sort order will be automatically applied.

2. **Click** on the **AZ button** to change the sort order to descending, if desired.

3. **Repeat steps 1** and **2** until you select all sort orders.

4. **Click** on **Next** to continue.

Specifying Summary Options

In the same wizard step in which you set sort orders, you can also specify summary options. In the Summary Options dialog box, you'll see a grid with check boxes that lets you specify up to four different summary options for each numeric field. These options include the ability to summarize a field as well as to display its average, minimum, or maximum.

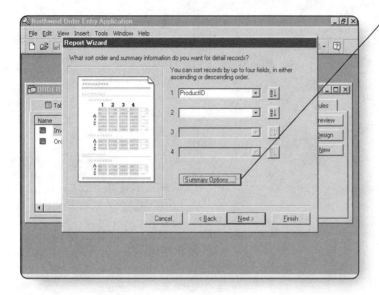

1. **Click** on the **Summary Options button**. The Summary Options dialog box will open.

2. **Click** on the **check box** for each field and summary option combination you want to include in your report.

3a. **Click** on the **Detail and Summary option button** to display both detail and summary information in your report.

OR

3b. **Click** on the **Summary Only option button** to display just the summary information in the report.

4. **Click** on the **Calculate percent of total for sums check box** to display the percentage of the total this amount represents.

5. **Click** on **OK**.

CAUTION

The Summary Options button won't appear in this step if your report doesn't include any numeric fields.

SPECIFYING THE REPORT LAYOUT

Next, you can choose the report layout you prefer from a selection of several different layouts. You can also set your report's orientation.

1. **Click** on the **layout option** you prefer in the Layout group box. A sample of the selected layout will display in the preview box.

2a. **Click** on the **Portrait option button** to display your report in portrait orientation.

OR

2b. **Click** on the **Landscape option button** to display in landscape orientation.

3. Click on the **Adjust the field width so all fields fit on the page check box**.

> ### NOTE
> By selecting the Adjust the field width so all fields fit on the page option, you will fit all the fields on one page, but some of these fields may truncate.

4. Click on **Next** to continue.

CHOOSING A REPORT STYLE

Access 97 includes six predefined report styles from which to choose.

1. Choose the **report style** you prefer from the list. A sample of the selected style will appear in the preview box.

2. Click on **Next** to continue.

FINISHING THE REPORT

In the final step of the Report Wizard, you'll create a report title and select the view you want to use when opening the report for the first time.

1. Enter a **name** for your report in the text box.

2a. **Click** on the **Preview the report option button** to open the report in Print Preview.

OR

2b. **Click** on the **Modify the report's design option button** to open the report in Design View.

NOTE

You can view a report in three ways: Design View, Layout Preview, and Print Preview. Design View lets you make changes to the report's design. Layout Preview gives you a basic view of the report's layout, but doesn't include all the data. Print Preview displays your report as it will look printed.

3. **Click** on the **Display Help on working with the report check box** if you want to display a help window when you open the report.

4. Click on **Finish**. The report will open based on your instructions in step 2.

If you open your report in Print Preview, you'll see exactly how it will look on paper.

If your final report isn't exactly what you want, you can customize it in Design View.

TIP

If you decide you want to start over again after creating a report, you can delete it by selecting it in the main database window and pressing the Delete key.

22 Changing a Report's Appearance

Once you create a report, you may want to change its default style or customize its formatting in other ways. In this chapter, you'll learn how to:

✦ Open a report in Design View

✦ Change a report's format

✦ Modify fonts

✦ Bold, italicize, and underline

✦ Set alignment

OPENING A REPORT IN DESIGN VIEW

You can open an existing report in Design View to modify its design.

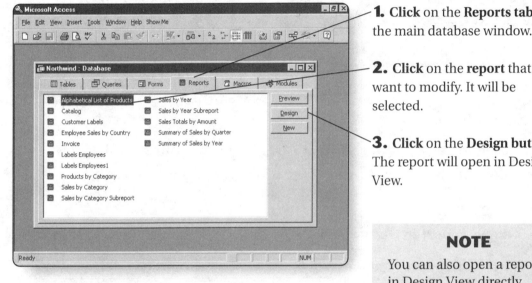

1. **Click** on the **Reports tab** in the main database window.

2. **Click** on the **report** that you want to modify. It will be selected.

3. **Click** on the **Design button**. The report will open in Design View.

NOTE

You can also open a report in Design View directly from the Report Wizard by choosing the Modify the report's design option button on the final wizard step.

When you look at a report in Design View, you'll see that an Access report consists of a number of controls placed in specific report sections.

Each report includes the following sections:

✦ Report Header

✦ Page Header

✦ Detail

✦ Page Footer

✦ Report Footer

Reports can also include group headers and footers if you apply groupings to the reports.

Report controls are objects such as labels or text boxes. The Report Wizard and AutoReport features automatically create report sections and place controls in the appropriate location. You can also create or modify report controls manually.

CHANGING A REPORT'S FORMAT

When you create a report using the Report Wizard or AutoReport feature, you choose a style or AutoFormat to apply. This format uses predefined colors, borders, fonts, and font sizes designed to look good together and convey a specific image. If you don't like the AutoFormat you originally chose for your report, you can change it.

1. **Click** on the **AutoFormat** button. The AutoFormat dialog box will open with the current format highlighted.

2. **Click** on a **new report format** in the Report AutoFormat: list.

3. **Click** on **OK** to apply the new format.

Selecting Specific Formatting Options

By default, an AutoFormat applies to all the fonts, colors, and borders on a report. You can use the Options button on the AutoFormat dialog box to apply changes only to specific parts of the report.

1. **Click** on the **Options button**. The AutoFormat dialog box will extend to include the Attributes to Apply group box. All three attributes are selected by default.

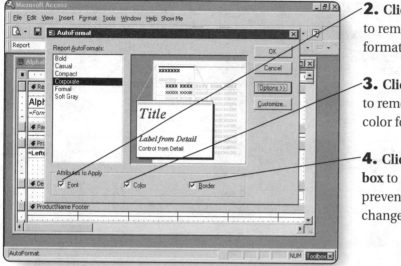

2. Click on the **Font check box** to remove the ✔ and prevent formatting changes to fonts.

3. Click on the **Color check box** to remove the ✔ and prevent color formatting changes.

4. Click on the **Border check box** to remove the ✔ and prevent border formatting changes.

CAUTION

Remember that Access AutoFormats and styles were designed to look good together. Making too many different font changes can make your report muddled or hard to read.

CHANGING FONTS

You can also change only the fonts in your report rather than the entire format or style. You can change the fonts of all report controls that contain text, such as labels or text boxes.

Changing Font Style

You'll use the Font drop-down list on the Formatting toolbar to change the font style of a selected control.

1. Click on the **control** whose font style you want to change. Handles will surround this control to indicate it is selected.

2. Choose the **new font** from the Font drop-down list on the Formatting toolbar.

The new font style will display in your report.

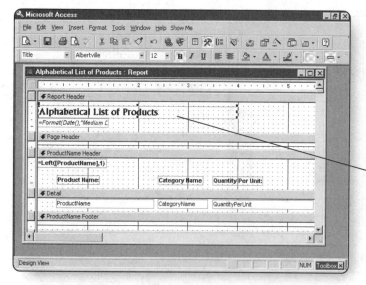

Changing Font Size

Use the Font Size drop-down list on the Formatting toolbar to modify the font size of a selected control.

1. Click on the **control** whose font size you want to change. Handles will surround this control to indicate it is selected.

2. Choose the **new font size** from the Font Size drop-down list on the Formatting toolbar.

NOTE

You can choose font sizes from 8 to 72 points.

The text now displays in the new font size.

Changing Font Color

You'll use the Font/Fore Color button on the Formatting toolbar to change font color in a report.

1. Click on the **control** whose font color you want to modify. Handles will surround this control to indicate it is selected.

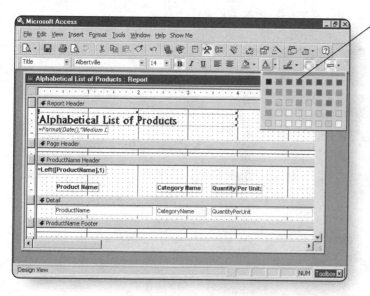

2. Click on the **down arrow** (▼)to the right of the Font/Fore Color button. The font color palette will open.

3. Click on the **color** you want to apply from the font color palette. The selected control will display in the new font color.

TIP

Click on the Font/Fore Color button itself to apply the default color that appears on the button.

BOLDING, ITALICIZING, AND UNDERLINING

In addition to changing the actual fonts in your report, you can modify them by bolding, italicizing, and underlining. These features are particularly useful when you want to emphasize something in your report. You can bold, italicize, and underline any control that includes text, such as a label or text box.

Bolding Text

You'll use the Bold button on the Formatting toolbar to bold text.

1. Click on the **control** you want to bold. It will be selected.

2. Click on the **Bold button**.

The text will display in bold.

Italicizing Text

You'll use the Italic button on the Formatting toolbar to ~~bold~~ text.

Italicize

1. Click on the **control** you want to italicize. It will be selected.

2. Click on the **Italic button**.

The text will be italicized.

Underlining Text

You'll use the Underline button on the Formatting toolbar to ~~bold~~ text.

Underline

1. **Click** on the **control** you want to underline. It will be selected.

2. **Click** on the **Underline button**.

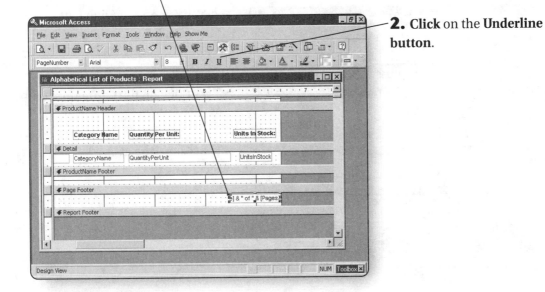

The text will be underlined.

SETTING ALIGNMENT

You can set left and center alignment on your Access reports using buttons on the Formatting toolbar.

1. Click on the **control** whose alignment you want to change.

2a. Click on the **Align Left button** to left align the text.

OR

2b. Click on the **Center button** to center the text.

The text will be aligned according to your instructions in step 2.

23 Printing Reports

You can print a report with the click of a button in Access 97, but the program also offers options for specifying exact report parameters. In this chapter, you'll learn how to:

✦ Open a report in Print Preview

✦ Print a default report

✦ Print a report with specific options

OPENING A REPORT IN PRINT PREVIEW

You can open an existing report in Print Preview to see how it will look before you print.

1. Click on the **Reports tab** in the main database window.

2. Click on the **report** you want to preview to select it.

3. Click on the **Preview button**. The report will open in Print Preview.

NOTE

You can also open a report in Print Preview directly from the Report Wizard by choosing the Preview the report option button on the final wizard step.

Zooming In on a Report

In Print Preview, the mouse pointer becomes a magnifying glass that you can use to zoom in and out of a specific area of the report for more detail. When you open a report, you will zoom in to the upper-left corner at 100%.

To display a full page view, click anywhere on the report.

To view a particular area in more detail, click on that part of the report. That area will display at 100%.

To increase or decrease the preview, choose a different zoom percentage from the Zoom list box on the Toolbar. You have several choices from 10% to 200%.

Navigating Through Report Pages

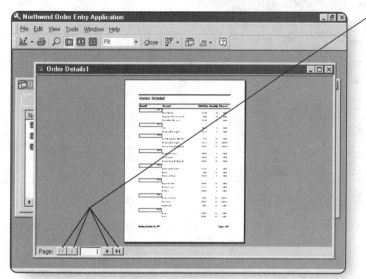

In the lower-left portion of the screen, you'll see four navigation buttons that enable you to move to the first, previous, next, and last page in the report.

PRINTING A DEFAULT REPORT

You can quickly and easily print a report using the default settings by clicking on the Print button in Print Preview.

NOTE

The Access 97 printing default is to print one copy of all pages of a report using the default printer you specified in Windows 95.

PRINTING A REPORT WITH SPECIFIC OPTIONS

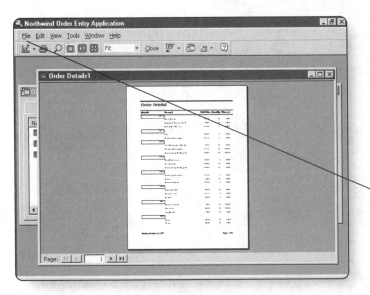

When you print a report, you may want to set options such as the specific pages and number of copies to print. If you have the capability to print to more than one printer, you'll want to be sure you specify the appropriate printer.

1. **Click** on **File**. The File menu will appear.

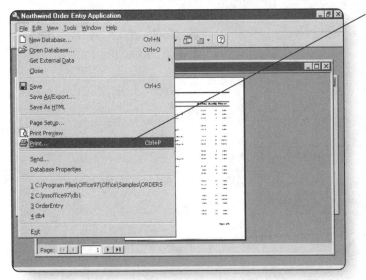

2. **Click** on **Print**. The Print dialog box will open.

3. Choose a **printer** from the Name: drop-down list.

4a. Click on the **All option button** in the Print Range group box to print all the pages in the report.

OR

4b. Click on the **Pages option button** and then enter the specific pages in the text boxes to print only selected pages.

5. Choose the **number of copies** to print from the Copies: scroll box.

6. Click on the **Collate check box** to collate multiple copies.

7. Click on **OK**. The report will print.

Setting Up Margins

You can also specify changes in the margins through the Print dialog box. Default margin settings are one inch on all sides—top, bottom, left, and right. These defaults work well in most circumstances, but if your report won't fit on a page, you may want to adjust the margins.

1. **Click** on the **Setup button**. The Page Setup dialog box will open.

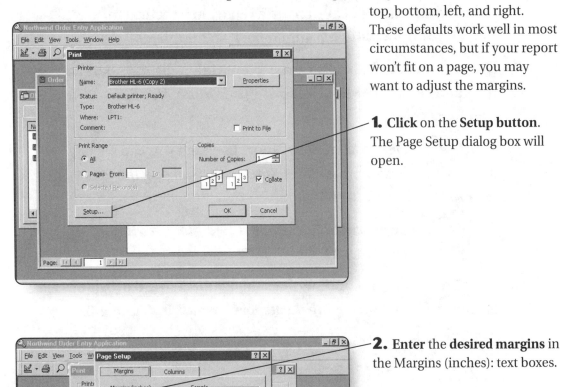

2. **Enter** the **desired margins** in the Margins (inches): text boxes.

3. **Click** on **OK**. You will return to the Print dialog box.

PART VII REVIEW QUESTIONS

1. How do you automatically create a report in a vertical format? *See "Creating a Columnar AutoReport" in Chapter 20*

2. How do you automatically create a report that displays data in rows and columns? *Flip to "Creating a Tabular AutoReport" in Chapter 20*

3. Which wizard lets you create a report in which you can specify many of your own parameters? *Start with "Starting the Report Wizard" in Chapter 21*

4. How do you specify report groupings? *Head to "Creating Groupings" in Chapter 21*

5. What kinds of layout options does the Report Wizard provide? *Browse through "Specifying the Report Layout" in Chapter 21*

6. In which view can you modify a report's design? *Look at "Opening a Report in Design View" in Chapter 22*

7. How can you apply a new report AutoFormat? *Learn in "Changing a Report's Format" in Chapter 22*

8. In which view can you see how a report will look before you print it? *Flip to "Opening a Report in Print Preview" in Chapter 23*

9. How can you view a report section in more detail? *Focus on "Zooming In on a Report" in Chapter 23*

10. Where can you specify the exact pages to print in a report? *Turn to "Printing a Report with Specific Options" in Chapter 23*

PART VIII

Working with the Web

roduc

ducts

roduct ID:

duct Name:

Supplier:

Category:

uantity Per Unit:

Unit Price:

Units In Stock:

Units On Order:

24 Adding Hyperlinks to the Web

Access 97 includes the ability to link data in tables and forms to documents on the Internet, your company's network, or your own computer hard drive through the use of *hyperlinks*. In this chapter, you'll learn how to:

✦ Add hyperlinks to a table in Design View

✦ Enter hyperlinks in tables

✦ Test your hyperlink

✦ Add a hyperlink column in Datasheet View

✦ Add a hyperlink label to a form

ADDING HYPERLINKS TO A TABLE IN DESIGN VIEW

In Access 97, you can include hyperlinks to the following:

✦ Documents on the Internet, such as a World Wide Web page

✦ Documents on your company network's Intranet site (internal Internet)

✦ Documents on your computer's hard drive, such as other Office 97 files

For example, in a table that stores customer information, you might want to include a field that links to each customer's Web site.

You can add a hyperlink field to a table in Design View.

1. Click on the **Tables tab** in the main database window.

2. Click on the **table you want to open**. It will be selected.

3. Click on the **Design button**. The table will open in Design View.

4. **Click** on the **row** beneath where you want to add a field. An arrow will appear in the field selector column.

5. **Click** on the **Insert Rows button**. A blank row will be added.

6. **Enter** the **name for the new field** in the Field Name column.

7. **Click** on the **field** whose data type you want to change in the Data Type column.

8. **Click** on the **down arrow** (▼) to the right of the Data Type column in the field row whose data type you want to change. A list box will appear.

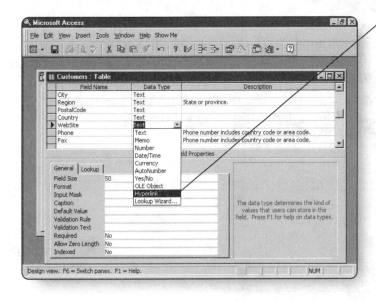

9. Click on the **new data type**.

10. Enter a **description** of the new hyperlink field, if desired.

11. Click on the **Close button.** A dialog box will ask if you want to save changes.

12. **Click** on **Yes**.

The table will close and save the changes.

ENTERING HYPERLINKS IN TABLES

After you add a hyperlink field to a table, you can enter the actual hyperlinks in Datasheet View. A hyperlink that you store in an Access table can have up to three parts:

+ **Display text**. The text you want to display in your hyperlink field. This is usually the name of the Web site.

+ **Address**. The URL of the site to which you want to link (http://www.microsoft.com) is an example of an address.

+ **Subaddress**. The exact location in the document or page to which you are linking. This is particularly useful when you are linking to another document on your computer, such as another Office 97 file. The subaddress could be a bookmark name in Word 97 or a slide number in PowerPoint 97, for example.

Access 97 requires the following format when entering a hyperlink: displaytext#address#subaddress. The address is required for a hyperlink field to work properly—the display text and subaddress are optional.

To enter a hyperlink in a table, you need to open it in Datasheet View.

1. Click on the **Tables tab** in the main database window.

2. Click on the **table** you want to open. It will be selected.

3. Click on the **Open button**. The table will open in Datasheet View.

4. Tab to the **field** in which you want to enter the hyperlink.

5. Enter the **display text** you want to appear in the field, if any.

NOTE

If you enter display text, the Edit Hyperlink dialog box will open instead. It's identical to the Insert Hyperlink dialog box.

6. Click on the **Insert Hyperlink button**. The Insert Hyperlink dialog box will open.

7. Enter the **hyperlink address** in the Link to File or URL: text box.

NOTE

If you entered display text, the display text will default in the Link to File or URL: text box. You must enter an actual hyperlink address in this text box to link to the World Wide Web, however.

TIP

Click on the Browse button for help in searching for a file that's located on your computer or company network.

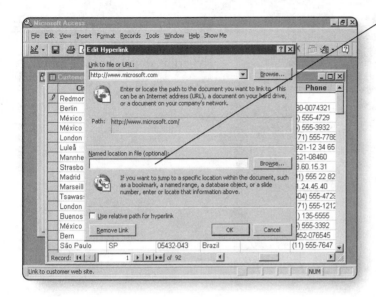

8. **Enter** the **subaddress**, if any, in the Named location in file (optional): text box.

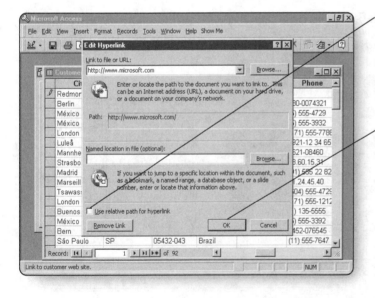

9. **Click** on the **Use relative path for hyperlink check box** to base the hyperlink on a relative path rather than an absolute path.

10. **Click** on **OK**.

NOTE

A hyperlink will display in colored, underlined text. This indicates that when you click on it, it will link you to the designated file or location.

If you entered a hyperlink address, the address will appear in the hyperlink field.

If you entered display text plus an address and/or subaddress, only the display text will appear.

To view the actual address to which the display text links, place the mouse pointer over the hypertext field without clicking. The hyperlink address will appear in the status bar.

TESTING YOUR HYPERLINK

To test the hyperlink you just added, double-click on the hyperlink.

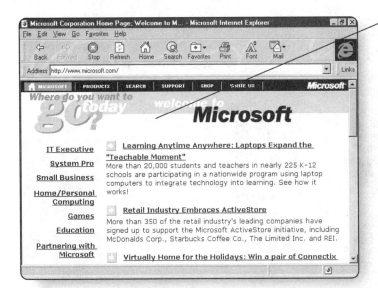

Your default browser will open and display the linked document or Web page.

If the hyperlink doesn't open properly or you receive an error message, you can modify it or delete it and enter a new hyperlink.

ADDING HYPERLINK COLUMNS IN DATASHEET VIEW

If you are already in Datasheet View, you can add a hyperlink column directly to the table datasheet.

1. Select the **field column** to the right of where you want to insert the hyperlink column.

2. Click on **Insert**. The Insert menu will appear.

3. Click on **Hyperlink Column**. A hyperlink field will be inserted to the left of the selected column.

When you save the changes, the new field will automatically be saved with the Hyperlink data type.

NOTE

If you use this shortcut method to add a hyperlink column, you must rename the column and then set any additional properties in Design View.

ADDING A HYPERLINK LABEL TO A FORM

You can also include hyperlink fields in forms. In general, a hyperlink field that exists in a table displays as any other field in a form.

NOTE

You can also include hyperlinks in reports, but you won't be able to use the hyperlink unless you export the report to a Word document, an Excel workbook, or HTML format.

In special cases, you might want to add a hyperlink label to the form header. This is a hyperlink that doesn't exist for each record in a table, but rather remains constant in the form header when you scroll through form records.

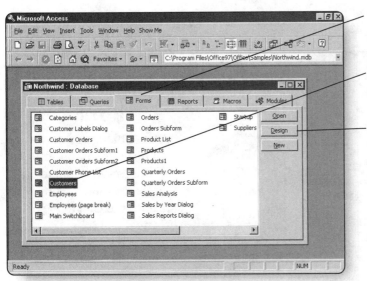

1. **Click** on the **Forms tab** in the main database window.

2. **Click** on the **form** you want to open. It will be selected.

3. **Click** on the **Design button**. The form will open in Design View.

4. **Click** on the **location on the form** where you want to place the hyperlink.

5. **Click** on the **Insert Hyperlink button**. The Insert Hyperlink dialog box will open.

6. **Enter** the **hyperlink address** in the Link to File or URL: text box.

NOTE

If you're linking to a document on your computer's hard drive rather than to an external document, you can leave the Link to file or URL: field blank.

TIP

Click on the Browse button for help in searching for a file that's located on your computer or company network.

7. Enter the **subaddress**, if any, in the Named location in file (optional): text box.

8. Click on the **Use relative path for hyperlink check box** to base the hyperlink on a relative path rather than an absolute path.

9. Click on **OK**.

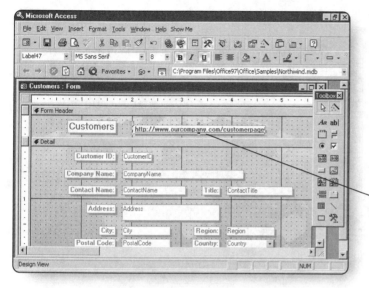

Renaming the Hyperlink Caption

The default caption for your hyperlink label will be the hyperlink address, but you can change this.

1. Double-click on the **hyperlink label**. The Label property box will open.

2. Enter a **new caption** in the Caption field.

3. Click on the **Close button**.

Click on the View button to preview the form in Form View. As you scroll through the form records, the hyperlink will remain constant in the form header.

25 Getting Support on the Web

You can connect directly to Microsoft's Web site from Access 97. On this site, you'll find a variety of useful tips that will help you get more out of Access. In this chapter, you'll learn how to:

✦ Access the Web tutorial

✦ Search for technical support

✦ Search for Access product news

✦ Search for free stuff

ACCESSING THE WEB TUTORIAL

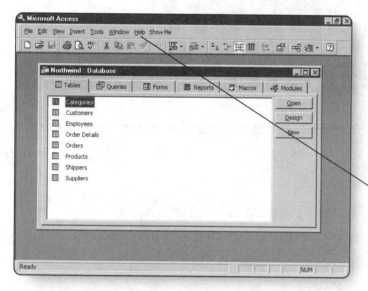

You can open Microsoft's Internet tutorial on the Web directly from Access 97. If you aren't comfortable with terms like URL and HTTP or want to know more about how the Internet and browsers work, this tutorial is a good place to start.

1. **Click** on **Help**. The Help menu will appear.

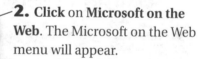

2. **Click** on **Microsoft on the Web**. The Microsoft on the Web menu will appear.

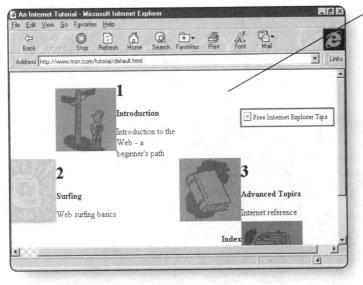

3. **Click** on **Web Tutorial**.

The tutorial contains three sections—an introduction, some how-to-surf instructions, and a reference area.

The Web tutorial on Microsoft's Web site will open using your default browser.

NOTE

Exactly how you access the Web from Access 97 will depend on your Internet connection. Connecting with a corporate network may be different from connecting with a home computer. For example, you may be required to complete a log-on procedure or you may connect directly without having to log on.

SEARCHING FOR TECHNICAL SUPPORT

If the Access 97 help features such as the Office Assistant, Help Index, or What's This? don't answer your questions, you can search Microsoft's Web site for additional technical support online. In general, the help topics on the Web site are more advanced than those within Access itself.

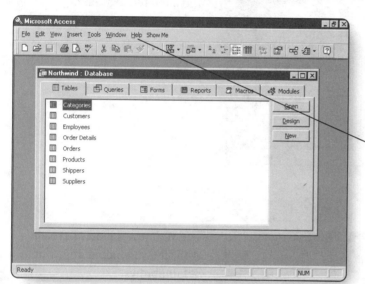

1. Click on **Help**. The Help menu will appear.

2. Click on **Microsoft on the Web**. The Microsoft on the Web menu will appear.

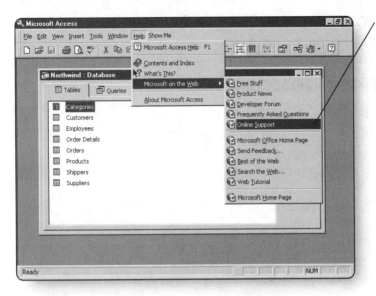

3. **Click** on **Online Support**. The Microsoft Technical Support page will open using your default browser.

4. **Choose Access** from the list box in step 1.

5. **Enter** a **question** in the text box in step 2.

6. **Click** on the **Find button**. A new Web page will open, displaying a numbered list of possible help topics.

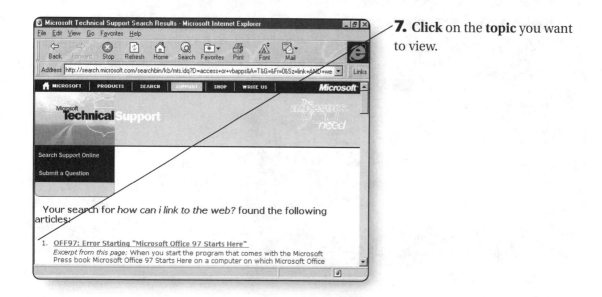

7. Click on the **topic** you want to view.

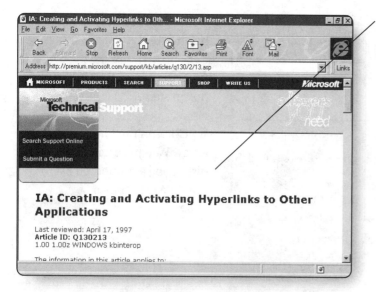

Detailed information on the topic you selected will display on a new Web page.

SEARCHING FOR ACCESS PRODUCT NEWS

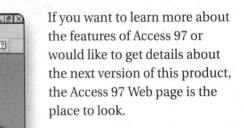

If you want to learn more about the features of Access 97 or would like to get details about the next version of this product, the Access 97 Web page is the place to look.

1. Click on **Help**. The Help menu will appear.

2. Click on **Microsoft on the Web**. The Microsoft on the Web menu will appear.

3. **Click** on **Product News**.

The Access 97 page on Microsoft's Web site will open using your default browser. This page includes product information as well as an animated mystery story that explains the mystery of relational databases in an easy-to-understand format.

SEARCHING FOR FREE STUFF

Microsoft's Web site also contains an area where you can obtain free software and tips about Access 97.

1. Click on **Help**. The Help menu will appear.

2. Click on **Microsoft on the Web**. The Microsoft on the Web menu will appear.

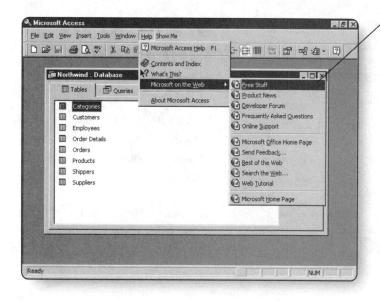

3. Click on **Free Stuff**.

The Free Stuff page will open using your default browser. As of the print date of this book, this page included free software downloads as well as other information and advice.

PART VIII REVIEW QUESTIONS

1. What are the three types of hyperlinks you can add to a table? *Find out in "Adding Hyperlinks to Tables in Design View" in Chapter 24*

2. What are the three parts of a hyperlink you can enter in a table? *See "Entering Hyperlinks in Tables" in Chapter 24*

3. How can you be sure your hyperlink will work properly? *Verify in "Testing Your Hyperlink" in Chapter 24*

4. What is the second way you can add a hyperlink to a table? *Flip to "Adding Hyperlink Columns in Datasheet View" in Chapter 24*

5. How do you include a hyperlink in a form? *Look at "Adding a Hyperlink Label to a Form" in Chapter 24*

6. Where do you change the form caption for a hyperlink? *Discover in "Renaming the Hyperlink Caption" in Chapter 24*

7. Where can you find Microsoft's Internet tutorial? *See "Accessing the Web Tutorial" in Chapter 25*

8. What can you do if you can't find the answer to your question in the Access online help? *Lean on "Searching for Technical Support" in Chapter 25*

9. How do you find out about the latest version of Access? *See "Searching for Access Product News" in Chapter 25*

10. Where can you find free software that you can use with Access? *Check through "Searching for Free Stuff" in Chapter 25*

PART IX

Appendixes

roduc

ducts

roduct ID:

duct Name:

Supplier:

Category:

uantity Per Unit:

Unit Price:

Units In Stock:

Units On Order:

A Creating Labels

The Access 97 Label Wizard lets you create a special kind of report that prints labels. In this chapter, you'll learn how to:

✦ **Start the Label Wizard**

✦ **Choose label size, font, and color**

✦ **Select label fields**

✦ **Specify sort options**

✦ **Finish the labels**

STARTING THE LABEL WIZARD

The Label Wizard guides you, step by step, through the creation of Avery style labels, such as mailing labels or rolodex cards.

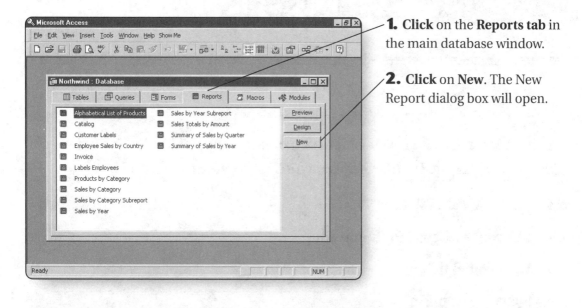

1. **Click** on the **Reports tab** in the main database window.

2. **Click** on **New**. The New Report dialog box will open.

3. **Click** on the **Label Wizard option**.

4. **Choose** the **table or query** on which you want to base your labels from the drop-down list.

5. **Click** on **OK**. The Label Wizard will open.

CHOOSING A LABEL SIZE

In the first wizard step, you make choices based on unit of measure and label type. A list of suitable Avery labels will then display.

1a. Click on the **English option button** to display English measurements.

OR

1b. Click on the **Metric option button** to display metric measurements.

2a. Click on the **Sheet feed option button** to display sheet feed label types.

OR

2b. Click on the **Continuous option button** to display continuous label types.

3. **Choose** the **label size** you need from the list.

4. **Click** on **Next** to continue.

CHOOSING LABEL FONT AND COLOR

In this step of the Label Wizard, you can specify fonts, colors, and text appearance. A sample of how your label will look appears in the preview box.

1. **Choose** the **font for your labels** from the Font Name: drop-down list.

2. **Choose** the **label font size** from the Font Size: drop-down list.

3. **Choose** the **font weight** from the Font Weight: drop-down list.

4. **Click** on the ... (**ellipsis**) **button** next to the Text Color: text box. The Color dialog box will open.

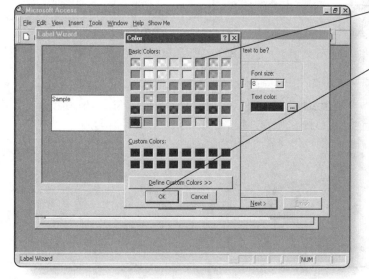

5. **Click** on the **color** you prefer from the Basic Colors: list.

6. **Click** on **OK** to return to the Label Wizard.

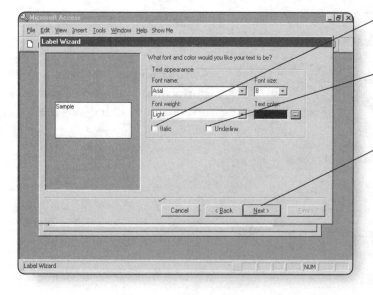

7. **Click** on the **Italic check box** to print the labels using italics.

8. **Click** on the **Underline check box** if you want to underline the label text.

9. **Click** on **Next** to continue to the next step.

SELECTING LABEL FIELDS

Next, you choose the specific fields to place on your labels, including the table or query in which they are located.

1. Click on the **first field** you want to include in your label from the Available fields: list.

2. Place the **mouse pointer** where you want to place the field in the Prototype label: text box.

3. Click on the **right arrow button**. The field will move to the Prototype label: text box.

TIP

To remove fields from the Prototype label, select them and then press the Delete key on your keyboard.

4. **Repeat steps 1** through **3** until you select all the fields you want to include on your label.

TIP

Be sure to include appropriate spaces and punctuation as you want them to appear on your labels. For example, you would want to include a space between the first and last name on a mailing label.

5. **Click** on **Next**. The Label Wizard will continue to the next step.

SPECIFYING SORT OPTIONS

You can sort the print order on one or more label fields.

1. Click on the **first field** on which you want to sort your report from the Available fields: list.

2. Click on the **right arrow button**. The field will move to the Sort by: list.

TIP

To remove a field from the Sort by: list, select it and then click on the left arrow button.

3. Repeat steps 1 and **2** until you select all required sort fields.

4. **Click** on **Next**. The Label Wizard will continue.

FINISHING THE LABELS

In the final step of the Label Wizard, you'll create a label report title and determine how you want to open your labels.

1. **Enter** a **name** for the label report in the text box.

2a. **Click** on the **See the labels as they will look printed option button** to open the labels in Print Preview.

OR

2b. **Click** on the **Modify the label design option button** to open the labels in Design View.

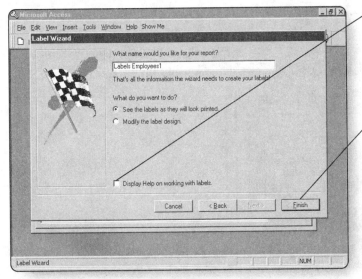

3. Click on the **Display Help on working with labels check box** if you want to display a help window when you open the labels.

4. Click on **Finish**. The labels will open based on your directions.

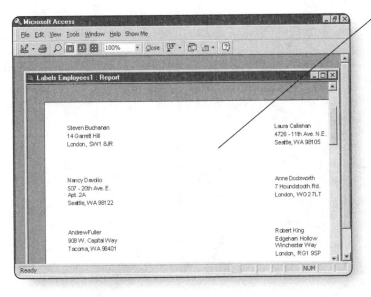

If you open the labels in Print Preview, you'll see how they will look when you print them. You print labels just as you would any other report, except that you must first load your printer tray with the appropriate labels.

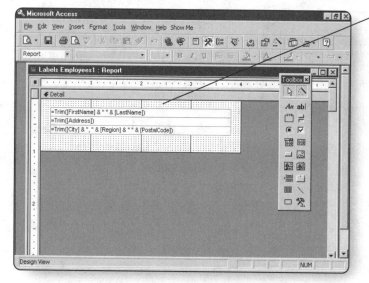

If you want to make further modifications to your labels, you can customize them in Design View.

B Importing Data from Excel

Using the Import Spreadsheet Wizard, you can quickly import existing worksheets from Excel 97. In this chapter, you'll learn how to:

✦ Start the import process

✦ Choose the worksheet to import

✦ Specify column headings

✦ Specify where to store data

✦ Set field options

✦ Define a primary key

✦ Finish the table

STARTING THE IMPORT PROCESS

The Import Spreadsheet Wizard will automate the process of importing an Excel 97 file, offering warnings about possible data compatibility problems when necessary.

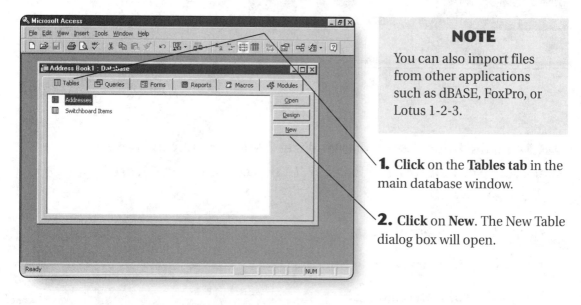

NOTE

You can also import files from other applications such as dBASE, FoxPro, or Lotus 1-2-3.

1. **Click** on the **Tables tab** in the main database window.

2. **Click** on **New**. The New Table dialog box will open.

3. **Click** on the **Import Table option**.

4. **Click** on **OK**. The Import dialog box will open.

5. Choose the **folder to display** from the Look in: list box.

6. Choose Microsoft Excel (*.xls) from the **Files of type: list box**. A list of Excel files will display.

7. **Click** on the **Excel file** that you want to import.

8. **Click** on the **Import button**.

The Import Spreadsheet Wizard will open.

CAUTION

If your workbook only contains one worksheet, this step of the wizard will not appear.

CHOOSING THE WORKSHEET TO IMPORT

First, you need to choose the worksheet or named range to import to an Access database. If your workbook contains several worksheets, you can only import one at a time. To help you choose the appropriate worksheet, sample data from the worksheet or named range will appear in the lower portion of the dialog box.

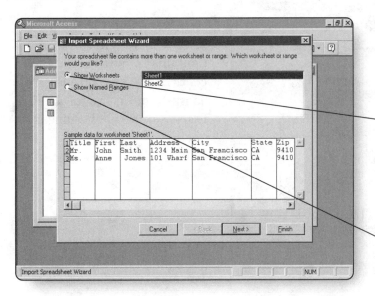

1a. **Click** on the **Show Worksheets option button** to display worksheets in the selected workbook.

OR

1b. **Click** on the **Show Named Ranges option button** to display named ranges in the selected workbook.

2. **Click** on the **worksheet or named range** you want to import.

3. **Click** on **Next**.

SPECIFYING COLUMN HEADINGS

You can use the first row of the selected Excel worksheet for your field names. Or, if the worksheet doesn't have column headings, you can create your own field names.

1. **Click** on the **First Row Contains Column Headings check box** if you want Access to consider the first row of your Excel worksheet as headings and not data.

2. **Click** on **Next** to continue.

SPECIFYING WHERE TO STORE DATA

You can store the data from the imported worksheet in either a new table or an existing Access table.

CAUTION

If you decide to store it in an existing table, be sure the Excel worksheet and Access table have the same structure. If they don't, you'll get an error message telling you that the import didn't work.

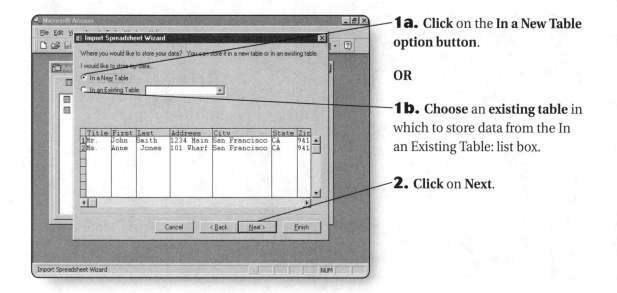

1a. **Click** on the **In a New Table option button**.

OR

1b. **Choose** an **existing table** in which to store data from the In an Existing Table: list box.

2. **Click** on **Next**.

SETTING FIELD OPTIONS

Next, you can modify field names and set indexing options. If you selected the First Row Contains Column Headings check box in an earlier step, the first worksheet row becomes the field names. If you didn't select this check box, the fields are named sequentially Field1, Field2, and so on, and you'll probably want to create more meaningful field names.

CAUTION

If you chose to import to an existing table in the previous step, this step won't appear. Instead, you'll move to the final wizard step where you can name your table.

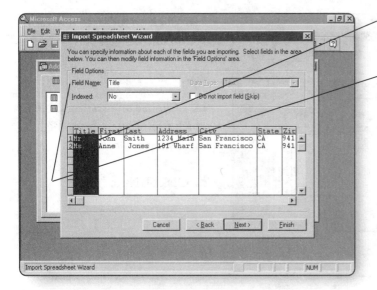

1. Click on the **first field** whose options you want to set.

2. Enter a **new name** for the field in the Field Name: text box, if desired.

3a. Click on **No** in the Indexed: list box if you don't want to index this field.

OR

3b. Click on **Yes (Duplicates OK)** in the Indexed: list box to index the field and allow duplicate entries.

OR

3c. Click on **Yes (No Duplicates)** in the Indexed: list box to index the field and not allow duplicate entries.

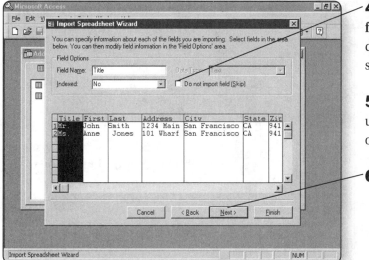

4. Click on the **Do not import field (Skip) check box** if you don't want to include the selected field in the Access table.

5. **Repeat steps 1** through **4** until you have finished creating options for all fields.

6. **Click** on **Next** to continue.

DEFINING A PRIMARY KEY

In this step of the Import Spreadsheet Wizard, you can define a *primary key*. This key provides a unique tag for each row in your table. Access uses the primary key to relate the records in this table to another table in your database.

CAUTION

If you chose to import to an existing table in an earlier step, this step won't appear. Instead, you'll move to the final wizard step where you can name your table.

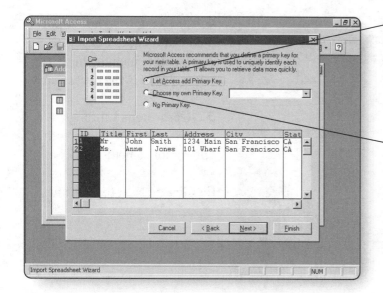

1a. Click on the **Let Access add Primary Key option button** to add a primary key field called ID.

OR

1b. Choose a **field** from the list box next to the Choose my own Primary Key option button to set an existing field as the primary key.

OR

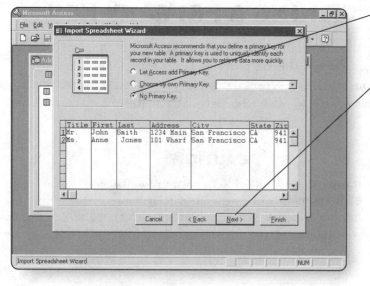

1c. Click on the **No Primary Key option button** to prevent setting a primary key.

2. Click on **Next** to continue to the next wizard step.

FINISHING THE TABLE

In the last step of the Import Spreadsheet Wizard, you specify a table name and set help options.

1. **Enter** a **name** for the new table in the Import to Table: text box if you are importing to a new table.

CAUTION

If you are importing to an existing table, the Import to Table: text box will automatically display this table name and you can't change it.

2. **Click** on the **I would like a wizard to analyze my table after importing the data check box**. The Table Analyzer Wizard will open after you finish.

NOTE

The Table Analyzer Wizard will analyze your table and provide suggestions and help on the best way to organize this information in Access 97.

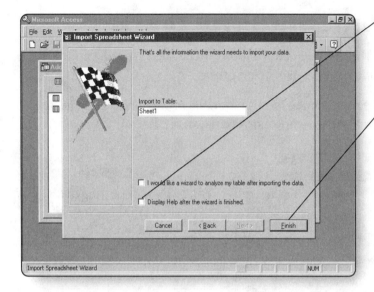

3. **Click** on the **Display Help after the wizard is finished check box** to open the help window.

4. **Click** on **Finish**.

The wizard will import the table based on the instructions you provided in this step.

Glossary

Address. The URL of the Web site to which you want to link. http://www.microsoft.com is an example of an address.

AutoForm. A basic automated form in either a columnar, tabular, or datasheet format.

AutoFormat. A way to automatically apply specific fonts, colors, and borders to a selected form or report.

AutoNumber. A data type which stores a unique incremented number for every record in a table.

AutoReport. A basic automated report in either a columnar or tabular format.

Browser. An external software program used to access and view World Wide Web pages. Microsoft Internet Explorer and Netscape Navigator are examples of browsers.

Check box. A control that lets you choose a particular option. A check mark in the check box indicates that the option is selected; no check mark indicates that it is not selected.

Click on. A way to perform an action by using the mouse to select a button, menu, or dialog box option.

Clipboard. A Windows holding area for transferring data.

Close button. A button you use to exit a dialog box, window, or Access itself.

Combo box. A control that contains a drop-down list from which you can select one of the listed values *or* enter a specific value not on the list.

Control. An object you place on a report or form. Text boxes, combo boxes, and option buttons are all examples of controls.

Criteria. Query and filter conditions that narrow the selected records or data.

Crosstab query. A query that summarizes information in a spreadsheet format by crosstabulating data.

Current record. The unique selected record that you can use or modify.

Data Entry mode. A mode that displays a blank table or form in which to enter data; temporarily hides all previously entered records from view.

Data type. A table field property that specifies the type of data you'll store in that field. Text, number, and date/time are examples of data types.

Database. A collection of information. In Access, objects such as forms, tables, reports, and queries make up a database.

Database window. A window that contains six tabs, each corresponding to one of the six objects that make up an Access database.

Datasheet View. A view that displays table data in rows and columns, as in a spreadsheet.

Default. A value that automatically displays in a field or control.

Design grid. The bottom portion of the Select Query window in which you specify query criteria.

Design View. A view that allows you to design or modify the selected report, table, form, or query.

Detail query. A select query that contains all fields in all records.

Dialog box. A box that displays when you perform another action, such as clicking on a button or menu option. A dialog box can either provide information or let you select additional options.

Display text. The text you want to display in a hyperlink field in a table.

Edit mode. A mode that allows you to enter data in a table or form; adds records to the end of existing records.

Field. A column in a table. An individual field relates specifically to the record with which it intersects.

Form. A database object you use to enter, view, and edit table data.

Filter by form. A feature that lets you filter based on more than one criterion.

Filter by selection. A feature that lets you select specific data in a table open in Datasheet View and then apply a basic filter.

Form section. A way to divide a form; an Access form can have detail, form header, page header, page footer, and form footer sections.

Form View. A view in which you can enter data in a form.

Hyperlink. In Access, a field data type that stores a link to a Web page or other object.

Hypertext Markup Language (HTML). A method of marking up or formatting documents for the World Wide Web.

Import. A method of transferring data from another source, such as a spreadsheet, into an Access table.

Internet. An international network of millions of computers.

Intranet. An internal corporate or organizational network that uses Internet technology.

Join lines. Lines in the Select Query window that relate data in one table to data in another.

Label. A control that displays descriptive text such as a title or caption.

Landscape. A page orientation that prints reports in a horizontal format.

List box. A control that contains a drop-down list from which you can select one of the listed values.

Menu bar. The horizontal bar located directly below the Access title bar that includes menu names.

Menu. A command list that displays when you click on a menu name on the menu bar.

Navigation buttons. Buttons that display in Datasheet and Form views that let you move to the first, last, next, and preceding records.

Office Assistant. A help feature that answers user questions.

Option group. A control that lets you choose one of several displayed options, preceded by option buttons, check boxes, or toggle buttons.

Portrait. A page orientation that prints reports in a vertical format.

Primary key. One or more table fields that serve as a unique tag for each table record; this unique key relates the records in the current table to records in other tables.

Print Preview. A view that displays a report as it will look when you print it.

Query. A database object that extracts specific information from a database; it can also perform an action on this data.

Record. A row in a table.

Report. A database object that presents or analyzes database information in a printed format.

Report section. A way to divide a report; an Access report can have detail, report header, page header, page footer, report footer, group header, and group footer sections.

ScreenTip. A tip that appears when you position the mouse pointer over a toolbar button or particular part of the screen.

Select query. A query that selects specific information from a database.

Sort. A command that organizes selected data in either ascending or descending order.

Style. A method of formatting objects using the same fonts, backgrounds, and colors.

Subaddress. The exact location in a Web page or document to which you want to link.

Summary query. A select query that summarizes information.

Table. A database object that serves as a collector of information about a related subject, organized by fields and records.

Text box. A control that you place on a form or report to display table or query data.

Title bar. The horizontal bar located directly above the menu bar which displays the name of the open window.

Toolbar. A horizontal bar located below the menu bar that includes toolbar buttons you click on to perform a specific action.

Toolbox. A toolbar that contains a series of buttons you use to create form or report controls.

Uniform Resource Locator (URL). The address of the Internet document, Web page, or object to which you want to link. http://www.microsoft.com is an example of a URL.

View. A window that lets you use an Access object in a particular way.

Wizard. An automated feature that guides you step-by-step through a process. In Access, you can use wizards to create databases, tables, reports, forms, and queries, for example.

World Wide Web. A graphical Internet environment accessed with a browser and organized with Web sites comprised of text, graphics, sound, and video.

Zoom. A way to reduce or enlarge the area you view in Print Preview.

Index

Notes

Notes

Notes

Send Us
YOUR COMMENTS

Dear Reader:

Thank you for buying this book. In order to offer you more quality books on the topics *you* would like to see, we need your input. At Prima Publishing, we pride ourselves on timely responsiveness to our readers needs. If you'll complete and return this brief questionnaire, *we will listen!*

Name: (first) _____ (M.I.) _____ (last) _____

Company: _____ Type of business: _____

Address: _____ City: _____ State: _____ Zip: _____

Phone: _____ Fax: _____ E-mail address: _____

May we contact you for research purposes? ❑ Yes ❑ No

(If you participate in a research project, we will supply you with your choice of a book from Prima CPD)

❶ How would you rate this book, overall?

❑ Excellent ❑ Fair
❑ Very Good ❑ Below Average
❑ Good ❑ Poor

❷ Why did you buy this book?

❑ Price of book ❑ Content
❑ Author's reputation ❑ Prima's reputation
❑ CD-ROM/disk included with book
❑ Information highlighted on cover
❑ Other (Please specify): _____

❸ How did you discover this book?

❑ Found it on bookstore shelf
❑ Saw it in Prima Publishing catalog
❑ Recommended by store personnel
❑ Recommended by friend or colleague
❑ Saw an advertisement in: _____
❑ Read book review in: _____
❑ Saw it on Web site: _____
❑ Other (Please specify): _____

❹ Where did you buy this book?

❑ Bookstore (name)_____
❑ Computer Store (name) _____
❑ Electronics Store (name) _____
❑ Wholesale Club (name) _____
❑ Mail Order (name) _____
❑ Direct from Prima Publishing
❑ Other (please specify): _____

❺ Which computer periodicals do you read regularly? _____
_____
_____

❻ Would you like to see your name in print?

May we use your name and quote you in future Prima Publishing books or promotional materials?

❑ Yes ❑ No

❼ Comments & Suggestions: _____
_____
_____

⑪ I would be interested in computer books on these topics

- ☐ Word Processing
- ☐ Database:
- ☐ Spreadsheets
- ☐ Networking
- ☐ Desktop Publishing
- ☐ Web site design
- Other _____

⑨ How do you rate your level of computer skills?

- ☐ Beginner
- ☐ Advanced
- ☐ Intermediate

⑩ What is your age?

- ☐ Under 18
- ☐ 18-24
- ☐ 25-29
- ☐ 30-39
- ☐ 40-49
- ☐ 50-59
- ☐ 60-over

⑧ Where do you use your computer?

	100%	75%	50%	25%
Work	☐	☐	☐	☐
Home	☐	☐	☐	☐
School	☐	☐	☐	☐

Other _____

PLEASE
PLACE
STAMP
HERE

PRIMA PUBLISHING
Computers & Technology Division
3875 Atherton Road
Rocklin, CA 95765

OTHER BOOKS FROM PRIMA PUBLISHING
Computers & Technology Division

ISBN	Title	Price
0-7615-1175-X	ACT! 3.0 Fast & Easy	$16.99
0-7615-0680-2	America Online Complete Handbook and Membership Kit	$24.99
0-7615-0417-6	CompuServe Complete Handbook and Membership Kit	$24.95
0-7615-0692-6	Create Your First Web Page In a Weekend	$29.99
0-7615-0743-4	Create FrontPage Web Pages In a Weekend	$29.99
0-7615-0428-1	The Essential Excel 97 Book	$27.99
0-7615-0733-7	The Essential Netscape Communicator Book	$24.99
0-7615-0969-0	The Essential Office 97 Book	$27.99
0-7615-0695-0	The Essential Photoshop Book	$35.00
0-7615-1182-2	The Essential PowerPoint 97 Book	$24.99
0-7615-1136-9	The Essential Publisher 97 Book	$24.99
0-7615-0752-3	The Essential Windows NT 4 Book	$27.99
0-7615-0427-3	The Essential Word 97 Book	$27.99
0-7615-0425-7	The Essential WordPerfect 8 Book	$24.99
0-7615-1008-7	Excel 97 Fast & Easy	$16.99
0-7615-1194-6	Increase Your Web Traffic In a Weekend	$19.99
0-7615-1191-1	Internet Explorer 4.0 Fast & Easy	$16.99
0-7615-1137-7	Jazz Up Your Web Site In a Weekend	$24.99
0-7615-1217-9	Learn Publisher 97 In a Weekend	$19.99
0-7615-1251-9	Learn Word 97 In a Weekend	$19.99
0-7615-1193-8	Lotus 1-2-3 Fast & Easy	$16.99
0-7615-0852-X	Netscape Navigator 3 Complete Handbook	$24.99
0-7615-1162-8	Office 97 Fast & Easy	$16.99
0-7615-0759-0	Professional Web Design	$40.00
0-7615-0063-4	Researching on the Internet	$29.95
0-7615-0686-1	Researching on the World Wide Web	$24.99
0-7615-1192-X	SmartSuite 97 Fast & Easy	$16.99
0-7615-1007-9	Word 97 Fast & Easy	$16.99
0-7615-1083-4	WordPerfect 8 Fast & Easy	$16.99
0-7615-1188-1	WordPerfect Suite 8 Fast & Easy	$16.99

TO ORDER BOOKS

Please send me the following items:

Quantity	Title	Unit Price	Total
_____	_____	$_____	$_____
_____	_____	$_____	$_____
_____	_____	$_____	$_____
_____	_____	$_____	$_____
_____	_____	$_____	$_____

Subtotal	$_____
Deduct 10% when ordering 3–5 books	$_____
7.25% Sales Tax (CA only)	$_____
8.25% Sales Tax (TN only)	$_____
5.0% Sales Tax (MD and IN only)	$_____
Shipping and Handling*	$_____
TOTAL ORDER	$_____

Shipping and Handling depend on Subtotal.

Subtotal	Shipping/Handling
$0.00–$14.99	$3.00
$15.00–29.99	$4.00
$30.00–49.99	$6.00
$50.00–99.99	$10.00
$100.00–199.99	$13.00
$200.00+	call for quote

Foreign and all Priority Request orders:
Call Order Entry department for price quote
at 1-916-632-4400

This chart represents the total retail price of books
only (before applicable discounts are taken).

By telephone: With Visa or MC, call 1-800-632-8676. Mon.–Fri. 8:30–4:00 PST.

By Internet e-mail: sales@primapub.com

By mail: Just fill out the information below and send with your remittance to:

PRIMA PUBLISHING

P.O. Box 1260BK

Rocklin, CA 95677-1260

http://www.primapublishing.com

Name_____ Daytime Telephone_____

Address _____

City _____ State _____ Zip_____

Visa /MC# _____Exp. _____

Check/Money Order enclosed for $_____ Payable to Prima Publishing

Signature_____